Charles Darwin's Works: The Formation of Vegetable Mould Through the Action of Worms

Charles Darwin, Sir Francis Darwin

THE FORMATION

OF

VEGETABLE MOULD

THROUGH THE

ACTION OF WORMS.

THE FORMATION

OF

VEGETABLE MOULD,

THROUGH THE

ACTION OF WORMS,

WITH

OBSERVATIONS ON THEIR HABITS.

BY

CHARLES Robert DARWIN, LL.D., F.R.S.

WITH ILLUSTRATIONS.

NEW YORK:

D. APPLETON AND COMPANY,

72 FIFTH AVENUE.

1896.

CONTENTS.

CHAPTER I.

HABITS OF WORMS.

CHAPTER II.

HABITS OF WORMS—*continued.*

CHAPTER III.

THE AMOUNT OF FINE EARTH BROUGHT UP BY WORMS TO THE SURFACE.

CHAPTER VI.

THE DENUDATION OF THE LAND—*continued.*

CHAPTER VII.

CONCLUSION.

THE

FORMATION OF VEGETABLE MOULD,

THROUGH THE ACTION OF WORMS, WITH OBSERVATIONS ON THEIR HABITS.

———•◦•———

INTRODUCTION.

THE share which worms have taken in the formation of the layer of vegetable mould, which covers the whole surface of the land in every moderately humid country, is the subject of the present volume. This mould is generally of a blackish colour and a few inches in thickness. In different districts it differs but little in appearance, although it may rest on various subsoils. The uniform fineness of the particles of which it is composed is one of its chief characteristic features; and this may be well observed in any gravelly country, where a recently-ploughed field

immediately adjoins one which has long remained undisturbed for pasture, and where
the vegetable mould is exposed on the sides
of a ditch or hole. The subject may appear
an insignificant one, but we shall see that
it possesses some interest; and the maxim
" de minimis lex non curat," does not apply
to science.   Even Elie de Beaumont, who
generally undervalues small agencies and
their accumulated effects, remarks.[*]   " la
" couche très-mince de la terre végétale est un
" monument d'une haute antiquité, et, par le
" fait de sa permanence, un objet digne d'oc-
" cuper le geologue, et capable de lui fournir
" des remarques intéressantes." Although
the superficial layer of vegetable mould as a
whole no doubt is of the highest antiquity,
yet in regard to its permanence, we shall hereafter see reason to believe that its component
particles are in most cases removed at not a
very slow rate, and are replaced by others
due to the disintegration of the underlying
materials.

As I was led to keep in my study during
many months worms in pots filled with earth,

[*] ' Leçons de Géologie Pratique,' tom. i. 1845, p. 140.

I became interested in them, and wished to learn how far they acted consciously, and how much mental power they displayed. I was the more desirous to learn something on this head, as few observations of this kind have been made, as far as I know, on animals so low in the scale of organization and so poorly provided with sense-organs, as are earth-worms.

In the year 1837, a short paper was read by me before the Geological Society of London,* "On the Formation of Mould," in which it was shown that small fragments of burnt marl, cinders, &c., which had been thickly strewed over the surface of several meadows, were found after a few years lying at the depth of some inches beneath the turf, but still forming a layer. This apparent sinking of superficial bodies is due, as was first suggested to me by Mr. Wedgwood of Maer Hall in Staffordshire, to the large quantity of fine earth continually brought up to the surface by worms in the form of castings. These castings are sooner or later

* 'Transactions Geolog. Soc.' vol. v. p. 505. Read November 1, 1837.

spread out and cover up any object left on the surface. I was thus led to conclude that all the vegetable mould over the whole country has passed many times through, and will again pass many times through, the intestinal canals of worms. Hence the term "animal mould" would be in some respects more appropriate than that commonly used of "vegetable mould."

Ten years after the publication of my paper, M. D'Archiac, evidently influenced by the doctrines of Elie de Beaumont, wrote about my "singulière théorie," and objected that it could apply only to "les prairies basses et humides;" and that "les terres labourées, les bois, les prairies élevées, n'apportent aucune preuve à l'appui de cette manière de voir." * But M. D'Archiac must have thus argued from inner consciousness and not from observation, for worms abound to an extraordinary degree in kitchen gardens where the soil is continually worked, though in such loose soil they generally deposit their castings in any open cavities or within their old burrows instead of on the surface. Von Hensen estimates that there are

* 'Histoire des progrès de la Géologie,' tom. i. 1847, p. 224.

about twice as many worms in gardens as in corn-fields.* With respect to "prairies élevées," I do not know how it may be in France, but nowhere in England have I seen the ground so thickly covered with castings as on commons, at a height of several hundred feet above the sea. In woods again, if the loose leaves in autumn are removed, the whole surface will be found strewed with castings. Dr. King, the superintendent of the Botanic Garden in Calcutta, to whose kindness I am indebted for many observations on earth-worms, informs me that he found, near Nancy in France, the bottom of the State forests covered over many acres with a spongy layer, composed of dead leaves and innumerable worm-castings. He there heard the Professor of "Aménagement des Forêts" lecturing to his pupils, and pointing out this case as a " beautiful example of the natural cultiva-" tion of the soil; for year after year the " thrown-up castings cover the dead leaves; " the result being a rich humus of great " thickness."

* 'Zeitschrift für wissenschaft. Zoologie,' B. xxviii. 1877 p. 361.

In the year 1869, Mr. Fish * rejected my
conclusions with respect to the part which
worms have played in the formation of vegetable mould, merely on account of their assumed
incapacity to do so much work. He remarks
that "considering their weakness and their
' size, the work they are represented to
" have accomplished is stupendous." Here we
have an instance of that inability to sum
up the effects of a continually recurrent
cause, which has often retarded the progress
of science, as formerly in the case of geology,
and more recently in that of the principle
of evolution.

Although these several objections seemed
to me to have no weight, yet I resolved to
make more observations of the same kind as
those published, and to attack the problem on
another side; namely, to weigh all the castings thrown up within a given time in a
measured space, instead of ascertaining the
rate at which objects left on the surface were
buried by worms. But some of my observations have been rendered almost superfluous
by an admirable paper by Von Hensen,

* 'Gardeners' Chronicle,' April 17, 1869, p. 418.

already alluded to, which appeared in 1877. Before entering on details with respect to the castings, it will be advisable to give some account of the habits of worms from my own observations and from those of other naturalists.

CHAPTER I.

HABITS OF WORMS.

Nature of the sites inhabited—Can live long under water—
Nocturnal—Wander about at night—Often lie close to the
mouths of their burrows, and are thus destroyed in large
numbers by birds—Structure—Do not possess eyes, but can
distinguish between light and darkness—Retreat rapidly when
brightly illuminated, not by a reflex action—Power of attention
—Sensitive to heat and cold—Completely deaf—Sensitive to
vibrations and to touch—Feeble power of smell—Taste—
Mental qualities—Nature of food—Omnivorous—Digestion—
Leaves before being swallowed, moistened with a fluid of the
nature of the pancreatic secretion—Extra-stomachal digestion
—Calciferous glands, structure of—Calcareous concretions
formed in the anterior pair of glands—The calcareous matter
primarily an excretion, but secondarily serves to neutralise the
acids generated during the digestive process.

EARTH-WORMS are distributed throughout the
world under the form of a few genera, which
externally are closely similar to one another.
The British species of Lumbricus have never
been carefully monographed; but we may
judge of their probable number from those
inhabiting neighbouring countries. In Scandinavia there are eight species, according to

Eisen;[*] but two of these rarely burrow in the ground, and one inhabits very wet places or even lives under the water. We are here concerned only with the kinds which bring up earth to the surface in the form of castings. Hoffmeister says that the species in Germany are not well known, but gives the same number as Eisen, together with some strongly marked varieties.[†]

Earth-worms abound in England in many different stations. Their castings may be seen in extraordinary numbers on commons and chalk-downs, so as almost to cover the whole surface, where the soil is poor and the grass short and thin. But they are almost or quite as numerous in some of the London parks, where the grass grows well and the soil appears rich. Even on the same field worms are much more frequent in some places than in others, without any visible difference in the nature of the soil. They abound in paved court-yards close to houses; and an instance will be given in which they had

---

[*] 'Bidrag till Skandinaviens Oligochætfauna,' 1871.

[†] 'Die bis jetzt bekannten Arten aus der Familie der Regenwürmer,' 1845.

burrowed through the floor of a very damp
cellar. I have seen worms in black peat in a
boggy field; but they are extremely rare, or
quite absent in the drier, brown, fibrous peat,
which is so much valued by gardeners. On
dry, sandy or gravelly tracks, where heath
with some gorse, ferns, coarse grass, moss and
lichens alone grow, hardly any worms can
be found. But in many parts of England,
wherever a path crosses a heath, its surface
becomes covered with a fine short sward.
Whether this change of vegetation is due to
the taller plants being killed by the occasional
trampling of man and animals, or to the soil
being occasionally manured by the droppings
from animals, I do not know.* On such
grassy paths worm-castings may often be seen.
On a heath in Surrey, which was carefully
examined, there were only a few castings on
these paths, where they were much inclined;

* There is even some reason to believe that pressure is actually
favourable to the growth of grasses, for Professor Buckman, who
made many observations on their growth in the experimental
gardens of the Royal Agricultural College, remarks ('Gardeners'
Chronicle,' 1854, p. 619): "Another circumstance in the cultivation of grasses in the separate form or small patches, is the
impossibility of rolling or treading them firmly, without which
no pasture can continue good."

but on the more level parts, where a bed of
fine earth had been washed down from the
steeper parts and had accumulated to a thickness of a few inches, worm-castings abounded.
These spots seemed to be overstocked with
worms, so that they had been compelled to
spread to a distance of a few feet from the
grassy paths, and here their castings had been
thrown up among the heath; but beyond this
limit, not a single casting could be found.   A
layer, though a thin one, of fine earth, which
probably long retains some moisture, is in
all cases, as I believe, necessary for their
existence; and the mere compression of the
soil appears to be in some degree favourable
to them, for they often abound in old gravel
walks, and in foot-paths across fields.

Beneath large trees few castings can be
found during certain seasons of the year, and
this is apparently due to the moisture having
been sucked out of the ground by the innumerable roots of the trees; for such places
may be seen covered with castings after the
heavy autumnal rains.   Although most cop-
pices and woods support many worms, yet in a
forest of tall and ancient beech-trees in Knole

Park, where the ground beneath was bare of all vegetation, not a single casting could be found over wide spaces, even during the autumn. Nevertheless, castings were abundant on some grass-covered glades and indentations which penetrated this forest. On the mountains of North Wales and on the Alps, worms, as I have been informed, are in most places rare; and this may perhaps be due to the close proximity of the subjacent rocks, into which worms cannot burrow during the winter so as to escape being frozen. Dr. McIntosh, however, found worm-castings at a height of 1500 feet on Schiehallion in Scotland. They are numerous on some hills near Turin at from 2000 to 3000 feet above the sea, and at a great altitude on the Nilgiri Mountains in South India and on the Himalaya.

Earth-worms must be considered as terrestrial animals, though they are still in one sense semi-aquatic, like the other members of the great class of annelids to which they belong. M. Perrier found that their exposure to the dry air of a room for only a single night was fatal to them. On the other hand he kept several large worms alive for nearly four months, completely submerged in water.* During the summer when the ground is dry, they penetrate to a considerable depth and cease to work, as they do during the winter when the ground is frozen. Worms are nocturnal in their habits, and at night may be seen crawling about in large numbers, but usually with their tails still inserted in their burrows. By the expansion of this part of their bodies, and with the help of the short, slightly reflexed bristles, with which their bodies are armed, they hold so fast that they can seldom be dragged out of the ground without being torn into pieces.† During the day they remain in their burrows, except at the pairing season, when those which inhabit adjoining burrows expose the greater part of their bodies for an hour or two in the early morning. Sick

---

* I shall have occasion often to refer to M. Perrier's admirable memoir, 'Organisation des Lombriciens terrestres' in 'Archives de Zoolcg. expér.' tom. iii. 1874, p. 372. C. F. Morren ('De Lumbrici terrestris,' 1829, p. 14) found that worms endured immersion for fifteen to twenty days in summer, but that in winter they died when thus treated.

† Morren, 'De Lumbrici terrestris,' &c., 1829, p. 67.

individuals, which are generally affected by the parasitic larvæ of a fly, must also be excepted, as they wander about during the day and die on the surface. After heavy rain succeeding dry weather, an astonishing number of dead worms may sometimes be seen lying on the ground. Mr. Galton informs me that on one such occasion (March, 1881), the dead worms averaged one for every two and a half paces in length on a walk in Hyde Park, four paces in width. He counted no less than 45 dead worms in one place in a length of sixteen paces. From the facts above given, it is not probable that these worms could have been drowned, and if they had been drowned they would have perished in their burrows. I believe that they were already sick, and that their deaths were merely hastened by the ground being flooded.

It has often been said that under ordinary circumstances healthy worms never, or very rarely, completely leave their burrows at night; but this is an error, as White of Selborne long ago knew. In the morning, after there has been heavy rain, the film of mud or of very fine sand over gravel-walks is often

plainly marked with their tracks. I have
noticed this from August to May, both months
included, and it probably occurs during the
two remaining months of the year when
they are wet. On these occasions, very few
dead worms could anywhere be seen. On
January 31, 1881, after a long-continued
and unusually severe frost with much snow,
as soon as a thaw set in, the walks were
marked with innumerable tracks. On one
occasion, five tracks were counted crossing
a space of only an inch square. They could
sometimes be traced either to or from the
mouths of the burrows in the gravel-walks,
for distances between 2 or 3 up to 15 yards.
I have never seen two tracks leading to the
same burrow; nor is it likely, from what we
shall presently see of their sense-organs, that
a worm could find its way back to its burrow
after having once left it. ˇ They apparently
leave their burrows on a voyage of discovery,
and thus they find new sites to inhabit.

Morren states * that worms often lie for
hours almost motionless close beneath the
mouths of their burrows. I have occasionally
noticed the same fact with worms kept in

* 'De Lumbrici terrestris,' &c., p. 14.

pots in the house; so that by looking down into their burrows, their heads could just be seen. If the ejected earth or rubbish over the burrows be suddenly removed, the end of the worm's body may very often be seen rapidly retreating. This habit of lying near the surface leads to their destruction to an immense extent. Every morning during certain seasons of the year, the thrushes and blackbirds on all the lawns throughout the country draw out of their holes an astonishing number of worms; and this they could not do, unless they lay close to the surface. It is not probable that worms behave in this manner for the sake of breathing fresh air, for we have seen that they can live for a long time under water. I believe that they lie near the surface for the sake of warmth, especially in the morning; and we shall hereafter find that they often coat the mouths of their burrows with leaves, apparently to prevent their bodies from coming into close contact with the cold damp earth. It is said that they completely close their burrows during the winter.

Structure.—A few remarks must be made on this subject. The body of a large worm consists of from 100 to 200 almost cylindrical rings or segments, each furnished with minute bristles. The muscular system is well developed. Worms can crawl backwards as well as forwards, and by the aid of their affixed tails can retreat with extraordinary rapidity into their burrows. The mouth is situated at the anterior end of the body, and is provided with a little projection (lobe or lip, as it has been variously called) which is used for prehension. Internally, behind the mouth, there is a strong pharynx, shown in the accompanying diagram (Fig. 1) which is pushed forwards when the animal eats, and this part corresponds, according to Perrier, with the protrudable trunk or proboscis of other annelids. The pharynx leads into the œsophagus, on each side of which in the lower part there are three pairs of large glands, which secrete a surprising amount of carbonate of lime. These calciferous glands are highly remarkable, for nothing like them is known in any other animal. Their use will be discussed when we treat of the digestive process. In most cf the species, the œsophagus is enlarged into a crop in front of the gizzard. This latter organ is lined with a smooth thick chitinous membrane, and is surrounded by weak longitudinal, but by powerful transverse muscles. Perrier saw these muscles in energetic action; and, as he remarks, the trituration of the food must be chiefly effected by this organ, for worms possess no jaws or teeth of any kind. Grains of sand and small stones, from the $\frac{1}{20}$ to a little more than the $\frac{1}{10}$ inch in diameter, may generally be found in their gizzards and intestines. As it is certain that worms swallow many little stones, independently of those swallowed while excavating their burrows, it is probable that they serve, like mill-stones, to triturate their food. The gizzard opens into the intestine,

Mouth.

Pharynx.

Œsophagus.

Calciferous glands.

Œsophagus.

Crop.

Gizzard.

Upper part of Intestine.

Fig. 1.

Diagram of the alimentary canal of an earthworm (Lumbricus), copied from Ray Lankester in 'Quart. Journ. of Microscop. Soc.' vol. xv. N.S. pl. vii.

which runs in a straight course to the vent at the posterior end of the body. The intestine presents a remarkable structure, the typhosolis, or, as the old anatomists called it, an intestine within an intestine; and Claparède[*] has shown that this consists of a deep longitudinal involution of the walls of the intestine, by which means an extensive absorbent surface is gained.

The circulatory system is well developed. Worms breathe by their skin, as they do not possess any special respiratory organs. The two sexes are united in the same individual, but two individuals pair together. The nervous system is fairly well developed; and the two almost confluent cerebral ganglia are situated very near to the anterior end of the body.

Senses.—Worms are destitute of eyes, and at first I thought that they were quite insensible to light; for those kept in confinement were repeatedly observed by the aid of a candle, and others out of doors by the aid of a lantern, yet they were rarely alarmed, although extremely timid animals. Other

---

[*] Histolog. Untersuchungen über die Regenwürmer. 'Zeitschrift für wissenschaft. Zoologie,' B. xix., 1869, p. 611.

persons have found no difficulty in observing worms at night by the same means.*

Hoffmeister, however, states † that worms, with the exception of a few individuals, are extremely sensitive to light; but he admits that in most cases a certain time is requisite for its action. These statements led me to watch on many successive nights worms kept in pots, which were protected from currents of air by means of glass plates. The pots were approached very gently, in order that no vibration of the floor should be caused. When under these circumstances worms were illuminated by a bull's-eye lantern having slides of dark red and blue glass, which intercepted so much light that they could be seen only with some difficulty, they were not at all affected by this amount of light, however long they were exposed to it. The light, as far as I could judge, was brighter than that from the full moon. Its colour apparently made no difference in the result. When they were

---

* For instance, Mr. Bridgman and Mr. Newman ('The Zoologist,' vol. vii. 1849, p. 2576), and some friends who observed worms for me.

† 'Familie der Regenwürmer,' 1845, p. 18.

illuminated by a candle, or even by a bright
paraffin lamp, they were not usually affected
at first. Nor were they when the light was
alternately admitted and shut off. Sometimes, however, they behaved very differently, for as soon as the light fell on them,
they withdrew into their burrows with
almost instantaneous rapidity. This occurred.
perhaps once out of a dozen times. When
they did not withdraw instantly, they often
raised the anterior tapering ends of their
bodies from the ground, as if their attention
was aroused or as if surprise was felt; or
they moved their bodies from side to side as
if feeling for some object. They appeared
distressed by the light; but I doubt whether
this was really the case, for on two occasions
after withdrawing slowly, they remained for
a long time with their anterior extremities
protruding a little from the mouths of their
burrows, in which position they were ready
for instant and complete withdrawal.

When the light from a candle was concentrated by means of a large lens on the
anterior extremity, they generally withdrew
instantly; but this concentrated light failed

to act perhaps once out of half a dozen trials. The light was on one occasion concentrated on a worm lying beneath water in a saucer, and it instantly withdrew into its burrow. In all cases the duration of the light, unless extremely feeble, made a great difference in the result; for worms left exposed before a paraffin lamp or a candle invariably retreated into their burrows within from five to fifteen minutes; and if in the evening the pots were illuminated before the worms had come out of their burrows, they failed to appear.

From the foregoing facts it is evident that light affects worms by its intensity and by its duration. It is only the anterior extremity of the body, where the cerebral ganglia lie, which is affected by light, as Hoffmeister asserts, and as I observed on many occasions. If this part is shaded, other parts of the body may be fully illuminated, and no effect will be produced. As these animals have no eyes, we must suppose that the light passes through their skins, and in some manner excites their cerebral ganglia. It appeared at first probable that the different manner in which they were affected on different occasions might be explained, either by the degree of extension of their skin and its consequent transparency, or by some particular incidence of the light; but I could discover no such relation. One thing was manifest, namely that when worms were employed in dragging leaves into their burrows or in eating them, and even during the short intervals whilst they rested from their work, they either did not perceive the light or were regardless of it; and this occurred even when the light was concentrated on them through a large lens. So, again, whilst they are paired, they will remain for an hour or two out of their burrows, fully exposed to the morning light; but it appears from what Hoffmeister says that a light will occasionally cause paired individuals to separate.

When a worm is suddenly illuminated and dashes like a rabbit into its burrow—to use the expression employed by a friend—we are at first led to look at the action as a reflex one. The irritation of the cerebral ganglia appears to cause certain muscles to contract in an inevitable manner, independently of the will

or consciousness of the animal, as if it were
an automaton. But the different effect
which a light produced on different occasions,
and especially the fact that a worm when in
any way employed and in the intervals of
such employment, whatever set of muscles
and ganglia may then have been brought into
play, is often regardless of light, are opposed
to the view of the sudden withdrawal being
a simple reflex action. With the higher
animals, when close attention to some object
leads to the disregard of the impressions
which other objects must be producing on
them, we attribute this to their attention
being then absorbed; and attention implies
the presence of a mind. Every sportsman
knows that he can approach animals whilst
they are grazing, fighting or courting, much
more easily than at other times. The state,
also, of the nervous system of the higher
animals differs much at different times, for
instance, a horse is much more readily startled
at one time than at another. The comparison
here implied between the actions of one of
the higher animals and of one so low in the
scale as an earth-worm, may appear far-

fetched; for we thus attribute to the worm attention and some mental power, nevertheless I can see no reason to doubt the justice of the comparison.

Although worms cannot be said to possess the power of vision, their sensitiveness to light enables them to distinguish between day and night; and they thus escape extreme danger from the many diurnal animals which prey on them. Their withdrawal into their burrows during the day appears, however; to have become an habitual action; for worms kept in pots covered by glass-plates, over which sheets of black paper were spread, and placed before a north-east window, remained during the day-time in their burrows and came out every night; and they continued thus to act for a week. No doubt a little light may have entered between the sheets of glass and the blackened paper; but we know from the trials with coloured glass, that worms are indifferent to a small amount of light.

Worms appear to be less sensitive to moderate radiant heat than to a bright light. I judge of this from having held at different

times a poker heated to dull redness near
some worms, at a distance which caused a
very sensible degree of warmth in my hand.
One of them took no notice; a second withdrew into its burrow, but not quickly; the
third and fourth much more quickly, and the
fifth as quickly as possible. The light from
a candle, concentrated by a lens and passing
through a sheet of glass which would intercept
most of the heat-rays, generally caused a
much more rapid retreat than did the heated
poker. Worms are sensitive to a low temperature, as may be inferred from their not
coming out of their burrows during a frost.

Worms do not possess any sense of hearing.
They took not the least notice of the shrill
notes from a metal whistle, which was repeatedly sounded near them; nor did they
of the deepest and loudest tones of a bassoon.
They were indifferent to shouts, if care was
taken that the breath did not strike them.
When placed on a table close to the keys of
a piano, which was played as loudly as
possible, they remained perfectly quiet.

Although they are indifferent to undula-
tions in the air audible by us, they are

extremely sensitive to vibrations in any solid object. When the pots containing two worms which had remained quite indifferent to the sound of the piano, were placed on this instrument, and the note C in the bass clef was struck, both instantly retreated into their burrows. After a time they emerged, and when G above the line in the treble clef was struck they again retreated. Under similar circumstances on another night one worm dashed into its burrow on a very high note being struck only once, and the other worm when C in the treble clef was struck. On these occasions the worms were not touching the sides of the pots, which stood in saucers; so that the vibrations, before reaching their bodies, had to pass from the sounding board of the piano, through the saucer, the bottom of the pot and the damp, not very compact earth on which they lay with their tails in their burrows. They often showed their sensitiveness when the pot in which they lived, or the table on which the pot stood, was accidentally and lightly struck; but they appeared less sensitive to such jars than to the vibrations of the piano; and their sensitiveness to jars varied much at different times. It has often been said that if the ground is beaten or otherwise made to tremble, worms believe that they are pursued by a mole and leave their burrows. I beat the ground in many places where worms abounded, but not one emerged. When, however, the ground is dug with a fork and is violently disturbed beneath a worm, it will often crawl quickly out of its burrow.

The whole body of a worm is sensitive to contact. A slight puff of air from the mouth causes an instant retreat. The glass plates placed over the pots did not fit closely, and blowing through the very narrow chinks thus left, often sufficed to cause a rapid retreat. They sometimes perceived the eddies in the air caused by quickly removing the glass plates. When a worm first comes out of its burrow, it generally moves the much extended anterior extremity of its body from side to side in all directions, apparently as an organ of touch; and there is some reason to believe, as we shall see in the next chapter, that they are thus enabled to gain a general

notion of the form of an object. Of all their
senses that of touch, including in this term
the perception of a vibration, seems much the
most highly developed.

In worms the sense of smell apparently is
confined to the perception of certain odours,
and is feeble. They were quite indifferent to
my breath, as long as I breathed on them very
gently. This was tried, because it appeared
possible that they might thus be warned of
the approach of an enemy. They exhibited
the same indifference to my breath whilst I
chewed some tobacco, and while a pellet of
cotton-wool with a few drops of mille-fleurs
perfume or of acetic acid was kept in my
mouth. Pellets of cotton-wool soaked in
tobacco juice, and in millefleurs perfume, and
in paraffin, were held with pincers and were
waved about within two or three inches of
several worms, but they took no notice. On
one or two occasions, however, when acetic
acid had been placed on the pellets, the worms
appeared a little uneasy, and this was
probably due to the irritation of their skins.
The perception of such unnatural odours
would be of no service to worms; and as such

timid creatures would almost certainly exhibit some signs of any new impression, we may conclude that they did not perceive these odours.

The result was different when cabbage-leaves and pieces of onion were employed, both of which are devoured with much relish by worms. Small square pieces of fresh and half-decayed cabbage-leaves and of onion bulbs were on nine occasions buried in my pots, beneath about ¼ of an inch of common garden soil; and they were always discovered by the worms. One bit of cabbage was discovered and removed in the course of two hours; three were removed by the next morning, that is, after a single night; two others after two nights; and the seventh bit after three nights. Two pieces of onion were discovered and removed after three nights. Bits of fresh raw meat, of which worms are very fond, were buried, and were not discovered within forty-eight hours, during which time they had not become putrid. The earth above the various buried objects was generally pressed down only slightly, so as not to prevent the emission of any odour.

On two occasions, however, the surface was
well watered, and was thus rendered somewhat compact. After the bits of cabbage and
onion had been removed, I looked beneath
them to see whether the worms had accidentally come up from below, but there was
no sign of a burrow; and twice the buried
objects were laid on pieces of tin-foil which
were not in the least displaced. It is of
course possible that the worms whilst moving
about on the surface of the ground, with their
tails affixed within their burrows, may have
poked their heads into the places where the
above objects were buried; but I have never
seen worms acting in this manner. Some
pieces of cabbage-leaf and of onion were twice
buried beneath very fine ferruginous sand,
which was slightly pressed down and well
watered, so as to be rendered very compact,
and these pieces were never discovered. On
a third occasion the same kind of sand was
neither pressed down nor watered, and the
pieces of cabbage were discovered and removed after the second night. These several
facts indicate that worms possess some power
of smell; and that they discover by this

means odoriferous and much-coveted kinds
of food.

It may be presumed that all animals which
feed on various substances possess the sense
of taste, and this is certainly the case with
worms. Cabbage-leaves are much liked by
worms; and it appears that they can distinguish between different varieties; but this
may perhaps be owing to differences in their
texture. On eleven occasions pieces of the
fresh leaves of a common green variety and
of the red variety used for pickling were
given them, and they preferred the green,
the red being either wholly neglected or much
less gnawed. On two other occasions, however, they seemed to prefer the red. Half-
decayed leaves of the red variety and fresh
leaves of the green were attacked about
equally. When leaves of the cabbage, horse-
radish (a favourite food) and of the onion were
given together, the latter were always and
manifestly preferred. Leaves of the cabbage,
lime-tree, Ampelopis, parsnip (Pastinaca), and
celery (Apium) were likewise given together;
and those of the celery were first eaten. But
when leaves of cabbage, turnip, beet, celery,

wild cherry and carrots were given together, the two latter kinds, especially those of the carrot, were preferred to all the others, including those of celery. It was also manifest after many trials that wild cherry leaves were greatly preferred to those of the lime-tree and hazel (Corylus). According to Mr. Bridgman the half-decayed leaves of *Phlox verna* are particularly liked by worms.[*]

Pieces of the leaves of cabbage, turnip, horse-radish and onion were left on the pots during 22 days, and were all attacked and had to be renewed; but during the whole of this time leaves of an Artemisia and of the culinary sage, thyme and mint, mingled with the above leaves, were quite neglected excepting those of the mint, which were occasionally and very slightly nibbled. These latter four kinds of leaves do not differ in texture in a manner which could make them disagreeable to worms; they all have a strong taste, but so have the four first mentioned kinds of leaves; and the wide difference in the result must be attributed to a preference by the worms for one taste over another.

[*] 'The Zoologist,' vol. vii. 1849, p. 2576.

Mental Qualities.—There is little to be said on this head. We have seen that worms are timid. It may be doubted whether they suffer as much pain when injured, as they seem to express by their contortions. Judging by their eagerness for certain kinds of food, they must enjoy the pleasure of eating. Their sexual passion is strong enough to overcome for a time their dread of light. They perhaps have a trace of social feeling, for they are not disturbed by crawling over each other's bodies, and they sometimes lie in contact. According to Hoffmeister they pass the winter either singly or rolled up with others into a ball at the bottom of their burrows.* Although worms are so remarkably deficient in the several sense-organs, this does not necessarily preclude intelligence, as we know from such cases as those of Laura Bridgman; and we have seen that when their attention is engaged, they neglect impressions to which they would otherwise have attended; and attention indicates the presence of a mind of some kind. They are also much more easily excited at certain times than at others.

* 'Familie der Regenwürmer,' p. 13.

They perform a few actions instinctively, that is, all the individuals, including the young, perform such actions in nearly the same fashion. This is shown by the manner in which the species of Perichæta eject their castings, so as to construct towers; also by the manner in which the burrows of the common earth-worm are smoothly lined with fine earth and often with little stones, and the mouths of their burrows with leaves. One of their strongest instincts is the plugging up the mouths of their burrows with various objects; and very young worms act in this manner. But some degree of intelligence appears, as we shall see in the next chapter, to be exhibited in this work,—a result which has surprised me more than anything else in regard to worms.

Food and Digestion.—Worms are omnivorous. They swallow an enormous quantity of earth, out of which they extract any digestible matter which it may contain; but to this subject I must recur. They also consume a large number of half-decayed leaves of all kinds, excepting a few which have an unpleasant taste or are too tough for them;

likewise petioles, peduncles and decayed flowers. But they will also consume fresh leaves, as I have found by repeated trials. According to Morren* they will eat particles of sugar and liquorice; and the worms which I kept drew many bits of dry starch into their burrows, and a large bit had its angles well rounded by the fluid poured out of their mouths. But as they often drag particles of soft stone, such as of chalk, into their burrows, I feel some doubt whether the starch was used as food. Pieces of raw and roasted meat were fixed several times by long pins to the surface of the soil in my pots, and night after night the worms could be seen tugging at them, with the edges of the pieces engulfed in their mouths, so that much was consumed. Raw fat seems to be preferred even to raw meat or to any other substance which was given them, and much was consumed. They are cannibals, for the two halves of a dead worm placed in two of the pots were dragged into the burrows and. gnawed; but as far as I could judge, they prefer fresh to putrid meat, and in so far I differ from Hoffmeister.

* 'De Lumbrici terrestris' p. 19.

Léon Frédéricq states[*] that the digestive fluid of worms is of the same nature as the pancreatic secretion of the higher animals; and this conclusion agrees perfectly with the kinds of food which worms consume. Pancreatic juice emulsifies fat, and we have just seen how greedily worms devour fat; it dissolves fibrin, and worms eat raw meat; it converts starch into grape-sugar with wonderful rapidity, and we shall presently show that the digestive fluid of worms acts on starch.[†] But they live chiefly on half-decayed leaves; and these would be useless to them unless they could digest the cellulose forming the cell-walls; for it is well known that all other nutritious substances are almost completely withdrawn from leaves, shortly before they fall off. It has, however, now been ascertained that cellulose, though very little or not at all attacked by the gastric secretion of the higher animals, is acted on by that from the pancreas.[‡]

---

[*] 'Archives de Zoologie expérimentale,' tom. vii. 1878, p. 394.

[†] On the action of the pancreatic ferment, see 'A Text-Book of Physiology,' by Michael Foster, 2nd edit. pp. 198–203. 1878.

[‡] Schmulewitsch, 'Action des Sucs digestifs sur la Cellulose.' Bull. de l'Acad. Imp. de St. Pétersbourg, tom. xxv. p. 549. 1879.

The half-decayed or fresh leaves which worms intend to devour, are dragged into the mouths of their burrows to a depth of from one to three inches, and are then moistened with a secreted fluid. It has been assumed that this fluid serves to hasten their decay; but a large number of leaves were twice pulled out of the burrows of worms and kept for many weeks in a very moist atmosphere under a bell-glass in my study; and the parts which had been moistened by the worms did not decay more quickly in any plain manner than the other parts. When fresh leaves were given in the evening to worms kept in confinement and examined early on the next morning, therefore not many hours after they had been dragged into the burrows, the fluid with which they were moistened, when tested with neutral litmus paper, showed an alkaline reaction. This was repeatedly found to be the case with celery, cabbage and turnip leaves. Parts of the same leaves which had not been moistened by the worms, were pounded with a few drops of distilled water, and the juice thus extracted was not alkaline. Some leaves, however, which had been drawn

into burrows out of doors, at an unknown
antecedent period, were tried, and though still
moist, they rarely exhibited even a trace of
alkaline reaction.

The fluid, with which the leaves are bathed,
acts on them whilst they are fresh or nearly
fresh, in a remarkable manner; for it quickly
kills and discolours them. Thus the ends of
a fresh carrot-leaf, which had been dragged
into a burrow, were found after twelve hours
of a dark brown tint. Leaves of celery,
turnip, maple, elm, lime, thin leaves of ivy,
and occasionally those of the cabbage were
similarly acted on. The end of a leaf of
Triticum repens, still attached to a growing
plant, had been drawn into a burrow, and
this part was dark brown and dead, whilst the
rest of the leaf was fresh and green. Several
leaves of lime and elm removed from burrows
out of doors were found affected in different
degrees. The first change appears to be that
the veins become of a dull reddish-orange.
The cells with chlorophyll next lose more or
less completely their green colour, and their
contents finally become brown. The parts
thus affected often appeared almost black by

4

reflected light; but when viewed as a transparent object under the microscope, minute
specks of light were transmitted, and this
was not the case with the unaffected parts
of the same leaves. These effects, however, merely show that the secreted fluid is
highly injurious or poisonous to leaves; for
nearly the same effects were produced in from
one to two days on various kinds of young
leaves, not only by artificial pancreatic fluid,
prepared with or without thymol, but quickly
by a solution of thymol by itself. On one
occasion leaves of Corylus were much discoloured by being kept for eighteen hours in
pancreatic fluid, without any thymol. With
young and tender leaves immersion in human
saliva during rather warm weather, acted in
the same manner as the pancreatic fluid, but
not so quickly. The leaves in all these cases
often became infiltrated with the fluid.

Large leaves from an ivy plant growing
on a wall were so tough that they could not
be gnawed by worms, but after four days
they were affected in a peculiar manner by the
secretion poured out of their mouths. The
upper surfaces of the leaves, over which the

worms had crawled, as was shown by the dirt
left on them, were marked in sinuous lines.
by either a continuous or broken chain of
whitish and often star-shaped dots, about
2 mm. in diameter. The appearance thus presented was curiously like that of a leaf, into
which the larva of some minute insect had
burrowed. But my son Francis, after making
and examining sections, could nowhere find
that the cell-walls had been broken down or
that the epidermis had been penetrated.
When the section passed through the whitish
dots, the grains of chlorophyll were seen to
be more or less discoloured, and some of the
palisade and mesophyll cells contained
nothing but broken down granular matter.
These effects must be attributed to the trans-
udation of the secretion through the epidermis
into the cells.

The secretion with which worms moisten
leaves likewise acts on the starch granules
within the cells. My son examined some
leaves of the ash and many of the lime,
which had fallen off the trees and had been
partly dragged into worm-burrows. It is
known that with fallen leaves the starch-

grains are preserved in the guard-cells of the stomata. Now in several cases the starch had partially or wholly disappeared from these cells, in the parts which had been moistened by the secretion; while they were still well pre-served in the other parts of the same leaves. Sometimes the starch was dissolved out of only one of the two guard-cells. The nucleus in one case had disappeared, together with the starch-granules. The mere burying of lime-leaves in damp earth for nine days did not cause the destruction of the starch-granules. On the other hand, the immersion of fresh lime and cherry leaves for eighteen hours in artificial pancreatic fluid, led to the dissolution of the starch-granules in the guard-cells as well as in the other cells.

From the secretion with which the leaves are moistened being alkaline, and from its acting both on the starch-granules and on the protoplasmic contents of the cells, we may infer that it resembles in nature not saliva,* but pancreatic secretion; and we know from Frédéricq that a secretion of this

* Claparède doubts whether saliva is secreted by worms: see Zeitschrift für wissenschaft. Zoologie,' B. xix. 1869, p. 601.

kind is found in the intestines of worms. As the leaves which are dragged into the burrows are often dry and shrivelled, it is indispensable for their disintegration by the unarmed mouths of worms that they should first be moistened and softened; and fresh leaves, however soft and tender they may be, are similarly treated, probably from habit. The result is that they are partially digested before they are taken into the alimentary canal. I am not aware of any other case of extra-stomachal digestion having been recorded. The boa-constrictor bathes its prey with saliva, but this is solely for lubricating it. Perhaps the nearest analogy may be found in such plants as Drosera and Dionæa; for here animal matter is digested and converted into peptone not within a stomach, but on the surfaces of the leaves.

Calciferous Glands.—These glands (see Fig. 1), judging from their size and from their rich supply of blood-vessels, must be of much importance to the animal. But almost as many theories have been advanced on their use as there have been observers. They consist of three pairs, which in the common earth-worm debouch into the alimentary canal in advance of the gizzard, but posteriorly to it in Urochtæa and some other genera.* The two posterior pairs are formed by lamellæ, which according to Claparède, are diverticula from the œsophagus.† These lamellæ are coated with a pulpy cellular layer, with the outer cells lying free in infinite numbers. If one of these glands is punctured and squeezed, a quantity of white pulpy matter exudes, consisting of these free cells. They are minute, and vary in diameter from 2 to 6 μ. They contain in their centres a little excessively fine granular matter; but they look so like oil globules that Claparède and others at first treated them with ether. This produces no effect; but they are quickly dissolved with effervescence in acetic acid, and when oxalate of ammonia is added to the solution a white precipitate is thrown down. We may therefore conclude that they contain carbonate of lime. If the cells

---

* Perrier, ' Archives de Zoolog. expér ' July, 1874, pp. 416, 419.

† ' Zeitschrift für wissenschaft. Zoologie,' B. xix. 1869, pp. 603–606.

are immersed in a very little acid, they become more transparent, look like ghosts, and are soon lost to view; but if much acid is added, they disappear instantly. After a very large number have been dissolved, a flocculent residue is left, which apparently consists of the delicate ruptured cell-walls. In the two posterior pairs of glands the carbonate of lime contained in the cells occasionally aggregates into small rhombic crystals or into concretions, which lie between the lamellæ; but I have seen only one, and Claparède only a very few such cases.

The two anterior glands differ a little in shape from the four posterior ones, by being more oval. They differ also conspicuously in generally containing several small, or two or three larger, or a single very large concretion of carbonate of lime, as much as 1½ mm. in diameter. When a gland includes only a few very small concretions, or, as sometimes happens, none at all, it is easily overlooked. The large concretions are round or oval, and exteriorly almost smooth. One was found which filled up not only the whole gland, as is often the case, but its neck; so that it

resembled an olive-oil flask in shape. These
concretions when broken are seen to be
more or less crystalline in structure. How
they escape from the gland is a marvel; but
that they do escape is certain, for they are
often found in the gizzard, intestines, and
in the castings of worms, both with those
kept in confinement and those in a state of
nature.

Claparède says very little about the
structure of the two anterior glands, and he
supposes that the calcareous matter of which
the concretions are formed is derived from
the four posterior glands. But if an anterior
gland which contains only small concretions
is placed in acetic acid and afterwards
dissected, or if sections are made of such
a gland without being treated with acid,
lamellæ like those in the posterior glands
and coated with cellular matter could be
plainly seen, together with a multitude of
free calciferous cells readily soluble in acetic
acid. When a gland is completely filled with
a single large concretion, there are no free
cells, as these have been all consumed in
forming the concretion. But if such a con-

cretion, or one of only moderately large size
is dissolved in acid, much membranous matter
is left, which appears to consist of the remains
of the formerly active lamellæ. After the
formation and expulsion of a large concretion,
new lamellæ must be developed in some
manner. In one section made by my son, the
process had apparently commenced, although
the gland contained two rather large concretions, for near the walls several cylindrical
and oval pipes were intersected, which were
lined with cellular matter and were quite
filled with free calciferous cells. A great
enlargement in one direction of several oval
pipes would give rise to the lamellæ.

Besides the free calciferous cells in which
no nucleus was visible, other and rather
larger free cells were seen on three occasions;
and these contained a distinct nucleus and
nucleolus. They were only so far acted on
by acetic acid that the nucleus was thus
rendered more distinct. A very small concretion was removed from between two of the
lamellæ within an anterior gland. It was
embedded in pulpy cellular matter, with
many free calciferous cells, together with a

multitude of the larger, free, nucleated cells, and these latter cells were not acted on by acetic acid, while the former were dissolved. From this and other such cases I am led to suspect that the calciferous cells are developed from the larger nucleated ones; but how this is effected was not ascertained.

When an anterior gland contains several minute concretions, some of these are generally angular or crystalline in outline, while the greater number are rounded with an irregular mulberry-like surface. Calciferous cells adhered to many parts of these mulberry-like masses, and their gradual disappearance could be traced while they still remained attached. It was thus evident that the concretions are formed from the lime contained within the free calciferous cells. As the smaller concretions increase in size, they come into contact and unite, thus enclosing the now functionless lamellæ; and by such steps the formation of the largest concretions could be followed. Why the process regularly takes place in the two anterior glands, and only rarely in the four posterior glands is quite unknown. Morren says that these glands disappear

during the winter; and I have seen some
instances of this fact, and others in which
either the anterior or posterior glands were
at this season so shrunk and empty, that
they could be distinguished only with much
difficulty.

With respect to the function of the calciferous glands, it is probable that they primarily serve as organs of excretion, and
secondarily as an aid to digestion. Worms
consume many fallen leaves; and it is known
that lime goes on accumulating in leaves until
they drop off the parent-plant, instead of
being re-absorbed into the stem or roots, like
various other organic and inorganic substances.* The ashes of a leaf of an acacia
have been known to contain as much as
72 per cent. of lime. Worms therefore would
be liable to become charged with this earth,
unless there were some special means for its
excretion; and the calciferous glands are
well adapted for this purpose. The worms
which live in mould close over the chalk,
often have their intestines filled with this
substance, and their castings are almost white.

* De Vries, 'Landwirth. Jahrbücher,' 1881, p. 77.

Here it is evident that the supply of calcareous matter must be superabundant.
Nevertheless with several worms collected on
such a site, the calciferous glands contained
as many free calciferous cells, and fully as
many and large concretions, as did the
glands of worms which lived where there was
little or no lime; and this indicates that the
lime is an excretion, and not a secretion
poured into the alimentary canal for some
special purpose.

On the other hand, the following considerations render it highly probable that the
carbonate of lime, which is excreted by the
glands, aids the digestive process under
ordinary circumstances. Leaves during their
decay generate an abundance of various kinds
of acids, which have been grouped together
under the term of humus acids. We shall
have to recur to this subject in our fifth
chapter, and I need here only say that these
acids act strongly on carbonate of lime. The
half-decayed leaves which are swallowed in
such large quantities by worms would, therefore, after they have been moistened and
triturated in the alimentary canal, be apt to

produce such acids.   And in the case of
several worms, the contents of the alimentary
canal were found to be plainly acid, as shown
by litmus paper.   This acidity cannot be
attributed to the nature of the digestive fluid,
for pancreatic fluid is alkaline; and we have
seen that the secretion which is poured out of
the mouths of worms for the sake of pre-
paring the leaves for consumption, is likewise
alkaline.   The acidity can hardly be due to
uric acid, as the contents of the upper part of
the intestine were often acid.   In one case
the contents of the gizzard were slightly acid,
those of the upper intestines being more
plainly acid.   In another case the contents of
the pharynx were not acid, those of the
gizzard doubtfully so, while those of the intestine were distinctly acid at a distance of
5 cm. below the gizzard.   Even with the
higher herbivorous and omnivorous animals,
the contents of the large intestine are acid.
" This, however, is not caused by any acid
" secretion from the mucous membrane; the
" reaction of the intestinal walls in the larger
" as in the small intestine is alkaline.   It
" must therefore arise from acid fermentations

" going on in the contents themselves. . . .
" In Carnivora the contents of the coecum
" are said to be alkaline, and naturally the
" amount of fermentation will depend largely
" on the nature of the food."*

With worms not only the contents of the
intestines, but their ejected matter or the
castings, are generally acid. Thirty castings
from different places were tested, and with
three or four exceptions were found to be
acid; and the exceptions may have been due
to such castings not having been recently
ejected; for some which were at first acid,
were on the following morning, after being
dried and again moistened, no longer acid;
and this probably resulted from the humus
acids being, as is known to be the case, easily
decomposed. Five fresh castings from worms
which lived in mould close over the chalk,
were of a whitish colour and abounded with
calcareous matter; and these were not in
the least acid. This shows how effectually
carbonate of lime neutralises the intestinal
acids. When worms were kept in pots filled

* M. Foster, 'A Text-Book of Physiology,' 2nd edit. 1878.
p. 243.

with fine ferruginous sand, it was manifest
that the oxide of iron, with which the grains
of silex were coated, had been dissolved and
removed from them in the castings.

The digestive fluid of worms resembles in
its action, as already stated, the pancreatic
secretion of the higher animals; and in these
latter, "pancreatic digestion is essentially
"alkaline; the action will not take place
"unless some alkali be present; and the
"activity of an alkaline juice is arrested by
"acidification, and hindered by neutraliza-
"tion."[*]   Therefore it seems highly probable
that the innumerable calciferous cells, which
are poured from the four posterior glands
into the alimentary canal of worms, serve to
neutralise more or less completely the acids
there generated by the half-decayed leaves.
We have seen that these cells are instantly
dissolved by a small quantity of acetic acid,
and as they do not always suffice to neutralise the contents of even the upper part of
the alimentary canal, the lime is perhaps
aggregated into concretions in the anterior
pair of glands, in order that some may be

* M. Foster, *Ibid.* p. 200.

carried down to the posterior parts of the
intestine, where these concretions would be
rolled about amongst the acid contents. The
concretions found in the intestines and in the
castings often have a worn appearance, but
whether this is due to some amount of
attrition or of chemical corrosion could not
be told. Claparède believes that they are
formed for the sake of acting as mill-stones,
and of thus aiding in the trituration of the
food. They may give some aid in this way;
but I fully agree with Perrier that this must
be of quite subordinate importance, seeing
that the object is already attained by stones
being generally present in the gizzards and
intestines of worms.

CHAPTER II.

HABITS OF WORMS—*continued.*

Manner in which worms seize objects—Their power of suction—The instinct of plugging up the mouths of their burrows—Stones piled over the burrows—The advantages thus gained—Intelligence shown by worms in their manner of plugging up their burrows—Various kinds of leaves and other objects thus used—Triangles of paper—Summary of reasons for believing that worms exhibit some intelligence—Means by which they excavate their burrows, by pushing away the earth and swallowing it—Earth also swallowed for the nutritious matter which it contains—Depth to which worms burrow, and the construction of their burrows—Burrows lined with castings, and in the upper part with leaves—The lowest part paved with little stones or seeds—Manner in which the castings are ejected—The collapse of old burrows—Distribution of worms—Tower-like castings in Bengal—Gigantic castings on the Nilgiri Mountains—Castings ejected in all countries.

In the pots in which worms were kept, leaves were pinned down to the soil, and at night the manner in which they were seized could be observed. The worms always endeavoured to drag the leaves towards their burrows; and they tore or sucked off small fragments, whenever the leaves were suffi-

5

ciently tender.   They generally seized the thin edge of a leaf with their mouths, between the projecting upper and lower lip; the thick and strong pharynx being at the same time, as Perrier remarks, pushed forward within their bodies, so as to afford a point of resistance for the upper lip.   In the case of broad flat objects they acted in a wholly different manner.   The pointed anterior extremity of the body, after being brought into contact with an object of this kind, was drawn within the adjoining rings, so that it appeared truncated and became as thick as the rest of the body.   This part could then be seen to swell a little; and this, I believe, is due to the pharynx being pushed a little forwards.   Then by a slight withdrawal of the pharynx or by its expansion, a vacuum was produced beneath the truncated slimy end of the body whilst in contact with the object; and by this means the two adhered firmly together.*   That under these circumstances a vacuum was produced was plainly

* Claparède remarks (' Zeitschrift für wissenschaft. Zoolog. B. 19, 1869, p. 602) that the pharynx appears from its structure to be adapted for suction.

seen on one occasion, when a large worm
lying beneath a flaccid cabbage leaf tried to
drag it away; for the surface of the leaf
directly over the end of the worm's body
became deeply pitted. On another occasion
a worm suddenly lost its hold on a flat leaf;
and the anterior end of the body was momen-
tarily seen to be cup-formed. Worms can
attach themselves to an object beneath water
in the same manner; and I saw one thus
dragging away a submerged slice of an
onion-bulb.

The edges of fresh or nearly fresh leaves
affixed to the ground were often nibbled by
the worms; and sometimes the epidermis and
all the parenchyma on one side was gnawed
completely away over a considerable space;
the epidermis alone on the opposite side
being left quite clean. The veins were
never touched, and leaves were thus sometimes partly converted into skeletons. As
worms have no teeth and as their mouths
consist of very soft tissue, it may be presumed that they consume by means of suction
the edges and the parenchyma of fresh
leaves, after they have been softened by the

digestive fluid. They cannot attack such strong leaves as those of sea-kale or large and thick leaves of ivy; though one of the latter after it had become rotten was reduced in parts to the state of a skeleton.

Worms seize leaves and other objects, not only to serve as food, but for plugging up the mouths of their burrows; and this is one of their strongest instincts. Leaves and petioles of many kinds, some flower-peduncles, often decayed twigs of trees, bits of paper, feathers, tufts of wool and horse-hairs are dragged into their burrows for this purpose. I have seen as many as seventeen petioles of a Clematis projecting from the mouth of one burrow, and ten from the mouth of another. Some of these objects, such as the petioles just named, feathers, &c., are never gnawed by worms. In a gravel walk in my garden I found many hundred leaves of a pine-tree (*P. austriaca* or *nigricans*) drawn by their bases into burrows. The surfaces by which these leaves are articulated to the branches are shaped in as peculiar a manner as is the joint between the leg-bones of a quadruped; and if these surfaces

had been in the least gnawed, the fact would
have been immediately visible, but there was
no trace of gnawing. Of ordinary dicotyle-
donous leaves, all those which are dragged
into burrows are not gnawed. I have seen
as many as nine leaves of the lime-tree
drawn into the same burrow, and not nearly
all of them had been gnawed; but such
leaves may serve as a store for future consumption. Where fallen leaves are abundant, many more are sometimes collected
over the mouth of a burrow than can be
used, so that a small pile of unused leaves is
left like a roof over those which have been
partly dragged in.

A leaf in being dragged a little way into
a cylindrical burrow is necessarily much
folded or crumpled. When another leaf is
drawn in, this is done exteriorly to the first
one, and so on with the succeeding leaves; and
finally all become closely folded and pressed
together. Sometimes the worm enlarges the
mouth of its burrow, or makes a fresh one
close by, so as to draw in a still larger number
of leaves. They often or generally fill up the
interstices between the drawn-in leaves with

moist viscid earth ejected from their bodies,
and thus the mouths of the burrows are
securely plugged. Hundreds of such plugged
burrows may be seen in many places,
especially during the autumnal and early
winter months. But, as will hereafter be
shown, leaves are dragged into the burrows
not only for plugging them up and for food,
but for the sake of lining the upper part or
mouth.

When worms cannot obtain leaves, petioles,
sticks, &c., with which to plug up the mouths
of their burrows, they often protect them by
little heaps of stones; and such heaps of
smooth rounded pebbles may frequently be
seen on gravel-walks. Here there can be no
question about food. A lady, who was interested in the habits of worms, removed the
little heaps of stones from the mouths of
several burrows and cleared the surface of the
ground for some inches all round. She went
out on the following night with a lantern,
and saw the worms with their tails fixed in
their burrows, dragging the stones inwards
by the aid of their mouths, no doubt by
suction. "After two nights some of the

" holes had 8 or 9 small stones over
" them; after four nights one had about
".30, and another 34 stones."[*]   One stone
which had been dragged over the gravel-walk
to the mouth of a burrow weighed two
ounces; and this proves how strong worms
are. But they show greater strength in sometimes displacing stones in a well-trodden
gravel-walk; that they do so, may be inferred
from the cavities left by the displaced stones
being exactly filled by those lying over the
mouths of adjoining burrows, as I have myself observed.

Work of this kind is usually performed
during the night; but I have occasionally
known objects to be drawn into the burrows
during the day. What advantage the worms
derive from plugging up the mouths of their
burrows with leaves, &c., or from piling
stones over them, is doubtful. They do not
act in this manner at the times when they
eject much earth from their burrows; for their
castings then serve to cover the mouth.
When gardeners wish to kill worms on a

* An account of her observations is given in the 'Gardeners
Chronicle,' March 28th, 1868, p. 324.

lawn, it is necessary first to brush or rake away the castings from the surface, in order that the lime-water may enter the burrows.* It might be inferred from this fact that the mouths are plugged up with leaves, &c., to prevent the entrance of water during heavy rain; but it may be urged against this view that a few, loose, well-rounded stones are ill-adapted to keep out water. I have moreover seen many burrows in the perpendicularly cut turf-edgings to gravel-walks, into which water could hardly flow, as well plugged as burrows on a level surface. Can the plugs or piles of stones aid in concealing the burrows from scolopenders, which, according to Hoffmeister,† are the bitterest enemies of worms? Or may not worms when thus protected be able to remain with safety with their heads close to the mouths of their burrows, which we know that they like to do, but which costs so many of them their lives? Or may not the plugs check the free ingress, of the lowest stratum of air, when chilled by

---

* London's ' Gard. Mag.' xvii. p. 216, as quoted in the ' Catalogue of the British Museum Worms,' 1865, p. 327.

† ' Familie der Regenwürmer,' p. 19.

radiation at night, from the surrounding ground and herbage. I am inclined to believe in this latter view; firstly, because when worms were kept in pots in a room with a fire, in which case cold air could not enter the burrows, they plugged them up in a slovenly manner; and secondarily, because they often coat the upper part of their burrows with leaves, apparently to prevent their bodies from coming into close contact with the cold damp earth. But the plugging-up process may perhaps serve for all the above purposes.

Whatever the motive may be, it appears that worms much dislike leaving the mouths of their burrows open. Nevertheless they will reopen them at night, whether or not they can afterwards close them. Numerous open burrows may be seen on recently-dug ground, for in this case the worms eject their castings in cavities left in the ground, or in the old burrows, instead of piling them over the mouths of their burrows, and they cannot collect objects on the surface by which the mouths might be protected. So again on a recently disinterred pavement of a Roman villa at Abinger (hereafter to be described)

the worms pertinaciously opened their burrows almost every night, when these had
been closed by being trampled on, although
they were rarely able to find a few minute
stones wherewith to protect them.

*Intelligence shown by worms in their manner
of plugging up their burrows.*—If a man had to
plug up a small cylindrical hole, with such
objects as leaves, petioles or twigs, he would
drag or push them in by their pointed ends;
but if these objects were very thin relatively
to the size of the hole, he would probably
insert some by their thicker or broader ends.
The guide in his case would be intelligence.
It seemed therefore worth while to observe
carefully how worms dragged leaves into
their burrows; whether by their tips or
bases or middle parts. It seemed more especially desirable to do this in the case of plants
not natives to our country; for although the
habit of dragging leaves into their burrows
is undoubtedly instinctive with worms, yet
instinct could not tell them how to act in
the case of leaves about which their progenitors knew nothing. If, moreover, worms
acted solely through instinct or an unvary-

ing inherited impulse, they would draw all kinds of leaves into their burrows in the same manner.   If they have no such definite instinct, we might expect that chance would determine whether the tip, base or middle was seized.   If both these alternatives are excluded, intelligence alone is left; unless the worm in each case first tries many different methods, and follows that alone which proves possible or the most easy; but to act in this manner and to try different methods makes a near approach to intelligence.

In the first place 227 withered leaves of various kinds, mostly of English plants, were pulled out of worm-burrows in several places. Of these, 181 had been drawn into the burrows by or near their tips, so that the foot-stalk projected nearly upright from the mouth of the burrow; 20 had been drawn in by their bases, and in this case the tips projected from the burrows; and 26 had been seized near the middle, so that these had been drawn in transversely and were much crumpled.   Therefore 80 per cent. (always using the nearest whole number) had been drawn in by the tip, 9 per cent. by the base or footstalk, and 11 per cent. transversely or by the middle. This alone is almost sufficient to show that chance does not determine the manner in which leaves are dragged into the burrows.

Of the above 227 leaves, 70 consisted of the fallen leaves of the common lime-tree, which is almost certainly not a native of England. These leaves are much acuminated towards the tip, and are very broad at the base with a well-developed foot-stalk. They are thin and quite flexible when half-withered. Of the 70, 79 per cent. had been drawn in by or near the tip; 4 per cent. by or near the base; and 17 per cent. transversely or by the middle. These proportions agree very closely, as far as the tip is concerned, with those before given. But the percentage drawn in by the base is smaller, which may be attributed to the breadth of the basal part of the blade. We here, also, see that the presence of a foot-stalk, which it might have been expected would have tempted the worms as a convenient handle, has little or no influence in determining the manner in which lime leaves are dragged into the burrows.

The considerable proportion, viz., 17 per cent., drawn in more or less transversely depends no doubt on the flexibility of these half-decayed leaves. The fact of so many having been drawn in by the middle, and of some few having been drawn in by the base, renders it improbable that the worms first tried to draw in most of the leaves by one or both of these methods, and that they afterwards drew in 79 per cent. by their tips; for it is clear that they would not have failed in drawing them in by the base or middle.

The leaves of a foreign plant were next searched for, the blades of which were not more pointed towards the apex than towards the base. This proved to be the case with those of a laburnum (a hybrid between *Cytisus alpinus* and *laburnum*) for on doubling the terminal over the basal half, they generally fitted exactly; and when there was any difference, the basal half was a little the narrower. It might, therefore, have been expected that an almost equal number of these leaves would have been drawn in by the tip and base, or a slight excess in favour of the latter. But of 73 leaves (not included in the first lot of 227) pulled out of worm-burrows, 63 per cent. had been drawn in by the tip; 27 per cent. by the base, and 10 per cent. transversely. We here see that a far larger proportion, viz., 27 per cent. were drawn in by the base than in the case of lime leaves, the blades of which are very broad at the base, and of which only 4 per cent. had thus been drawn in. We may perhaps account for the fact of a still larger proportion of the laburnum leaves not having been drawn in by the base, by worms having acquired the habit of generally drawing in leaves by their tips and thus avoiding the foot-stalk. For the basal margin of the blade in many kinds of leaves forms a large angle with the foot-stalk; and if such a leaf were drawn in by the foot-stalk, the basal margin would come abruptly into contact with the ground on each side of the burrow, and would render the drawing in of the leaf very difficult.

Nevertheless worms break through their habit of avoiding the footstalk, if this part offers them the most convenient means for drawing leaves into their burrows. The leaves of the endless hybridised varieties of the Rhododendron vary much in shape; some are narrowest towards the base and others towards the apex. After they have fallen off, the blade on each side of the midrib often becomes curled up while drying, sometimes along the whole length, sometimes chiefly at the base, sometimes towards the apex. Out of 28 fallen leaves on one bed of peat in my garden, no less than 23 were narrower in the basal quarter than in the terminal quarter of their length; and this narrowness was chiefly due to the curling in of the margins. Out of 36 fallen leaves on another bed, in which different varieties of the Rhododendron grew, only 17 were narrower towards the base than towards the apex. My son William, who first called my attention to this case, picked up 237 fallen leaves in his garden (where the Rhododendron grows in the natural soil) and of these 65 per cent. could have been drawn by worms into their burrows more easily by the base or foot-stalk than by the tip; and this was partly due to the shape of the leaf and in a less degree to the curling in of the margins: 27 per

cent. could have been drawn in more easily
by the tip than by the base : and 8 per cent.
with about equal ease by either end. The
shape of a fallen leaf ought to be judged
of before one end has been drawn into a
burrow, for after this has happened, the free
end, whether it be the base or apex, will dry
more quickly than the end embedded in the
damp ground ; and the exposed margins of
the free end will consequently tend to become
more curled inwards than they were when
the leaf was first seized by the worm. My
son found 91 leaves which had been dragged
by worms into their burrows, though not to a
great depth ; of these 66 per cent. had been
drawn in by the base or foot-stalk ; and 34
per cent. by the tip. In this case, therefore, the worms judged with a considerable
degree of correctness how best to draw the
withered leaves of this foreign plant into their
burrows ; notwithstanding that they had to
depart from their usual habit of avoiding
the foot-stalk.

On the gravel-walks in my garden a very
large number of leaves of three species of
Pinus (*P. austriaca, nigricans* and *sylvestris*)

are regularly drawn into the mouths of worm-
burrows. These leaves consist of two needles,
which are of considerable length in the two
first and short in the last named species, and
are united to a common base ; and it is by this
part that they are almost invariably drawn
into the burrows. I have seen only two or
at most three exceptions to this rule with
worms in a state of nature. As the sharply
pointed needles diverge a little, and as several
leaves are drawn into the same burrow, each
tuft forms a perfect *chevaux de frise*. On two
occasions many of these tufts were pulled up
in the evening, but by the following morning
fresh leaves had been pulled in, and the
burrows were again well protected. These
leaves could not be dragged into the burrows
to any depth, except by their bases, as a
worm cannot seize hold of the two needles at
the same time, and if one alone were seized
by the apex, the other would be pressed
against the ground and would resist the
entry of the seized one. This was manifest
in the above mentioned two or three excep-
tional cases. In order, therefore that worms
should do their work well, they must drag

pine-leaves into their burrows by their bases, where the two needles are conjoined. But how they are guided in this work is a perplexing question.

This difficulty led my son Francis and myself to observe worms in confinement during several nights by the aid of a dim light, while they dragged the leaves of the above named pines into their burrows. They moved the anterior extremities of their bodies about the leaves, and on several occasions when they touched the sharp end of a needle they withdrew suddenly as if pricked. But I doubt whether they were hurt, for they are indifferent to very sharp objects, and will swallow even rose-thorns and small splinters of glass. It may also be doubted, whether the sharp ends of the needles serve to tell them that this is the wrong end to seize; for the points were cut off many leaves for a length of about one inch, and fifty-seven of them thus treated were drawn into the burrows by their bases, and not one by the cut-off ends. The worms in confinement often seized the needles near the middle and drew them towards the mouths of their burrows; and one

worm tried in a senseless manner to drag
them into the burrow by bending them.
They sometimes collected many more leaves
over the mouths of their burrows (as in the
case formerly mentioned of lime-leaves) than
could enter them. On other occasions, however, they behaved very differently; for as
soon as they touched the base of a pine-leaf,
this was seized, being sometimes completely engulfed in their mouths, or a point very near
the base was seized, and the leaf was then
quickly dragged or rather jerked into their
burrows. It appeared both to my son and
myself as if the worms instantly perceived
as soon as they had seized a leaf in the proper
manner. Nine such cases were observed,
but in one of them the worm failed to drag
the leaf into its burrow, as it was entangled
by other leaves lying near. In another case
a leaf stood nearly upright with the points of
the needles partly inserted into a burrow, but
the worm there was not seen; and then the
worm reared itself up and seized the base.
It was dragged into the mouth of the
burrow by bending the whole leaf. On the
other hand, if a worm had seized the base

of a leaf, this was on two occasions relinquished from some unknown motive.

As already remarked, the habit of plugging up the mouths of the burrows with various objects, is no doubt instinctive in worms; and a very young one, born in one of my pots, dragged for some little distance a Scotch-fir leaf, one needle of which was as long and almost as thick as its own body. No species of pine is endemic in this part of England, it is therefore incredible that the proper manner of dragging pine-leaves into the burrows can be instinctive with our worms. But as the worms on which the above observations were made, were dug up beneath or near some pines, which had been planted there about forty years, it was desirable to prove that their actions were not instinctive. Accordingly, pine-leaves were scattered on the ground in places far removed from any pine-tree, and 90 of them were drawn into the burrows by their bases. Only two were drawn in by the tips of the needles, and these were not real exceptions, as one was drawn in for a very short distance, and the two needles of the other cohered. Other pine-leaves were given to worms kept in pots in a warm room, and here the result was different; for out of 42 leaves drawn into the burrows, no less than 16 were drawn in by the tips of the needles. These worms, however, worked in a careless or slovenly manner; for the leaves were often drawn in to only a small depth; sometimes they were merely heaped over the mouths of the burrows, and sometimes none were drawn in. I believe that this carelessness may be accounted for by the air of the room being warm, and the worms consequently not being anxious to plug up their holes effectually. Pots tenanted by worms and covered with a net which allowed the entrance of cold air, were left out of doors for several nights, and now 72 leaves were all properly drawn in by their bases.

It might perhaps be inferred from the facts as yet given, that worms somehow gain a general notion of the shape or structure of pine leaves, and perceive that it is necessary for them to seize the base where the two needles are conjoined. But the following cases make this more than doubtful. The tips of a large number of needles of *P. austriaca* were cemented together with shell-lac dissolved in alcohol, and were kept for some days, until, as I believe, all odour or taste had been lost; and they were then scattered on the ground where no pine-trees grew, near burrows from which the plugging had been removed. Such leaves could have been drawn into the burrows with equal ease by either end; and judging from analogy and more especially from the case presently to be given of the petioles of *Clematis montana*, I expected that the apex would have been preferred. But the result was that out of 121 leaves with the tips cemented, which were drawn into burrows, 108 were drawn in by their bases, and only 13 by their tips. Thinking that the worms might possibly perceive and dislike the smell or taste of the shell-lac, though this was very improbable, especially after the leaves had been left out during several nights, the tips of the needles of many leaves were tied together with fine thread. Of leaves thus treated 150 were drawn into burrows— 123 by the base and 27 by the tied tips; so that between four and five times as many were drawn in by the base as by the tip.   It is possible that the short cut-off ends of the thread with which they were tied, may have tempted the worms to drag in a larger proportional number by the tips than when cement was used.   Of the leaves with tied and cemented tips taken together (271 in number) 85 per cent. were drawn in by the base and 15 per cent. by the tips.   We may therefore infer that it is not the divergence of the two needles which leads worms in a state of nature almost invariably to drag pine-leaves into their burrows by the base.   Nor can it be the sharpness of the points of the needles which determines them; for, as we have seen, many leaves with the points cut off were drawn in by their bases.   We are thus led to conclude, that with pine-leaves there must be something attractive to worms in the base, notwithstanding that few ordinary leaves are drawn in by the base or footstalk.

Petioles.—We will now turn to the petioles or foot-stalks of compound leaves, after the leaflets have fallen off.   Those from *Clematis montana*, which grew over a verandah, were dragged early in January in large numbers

into the burrows on an adjoining gravel-
walk, lawn, and flower-bed.   These petioles
vary from 2½ to 4½ inches in length, are
rigid and of nearly uniform thickness, except
close to the base where they thicken rather
abruptly, being here about twice as thick as
in any other part.   The apex is somewhat
pointed, but soon withers and is then easily
broken off. Of these petioles, 314 were pulled
out of burrows in the above specified sites;
and it was found that 76 per cent. had been
drawn in by their tips, and 24 per cent. by
their bases; so that those drawn in by the
tip were a little more than thrice as many
as those drawn in by the base.   Some of those
extracted from the well-beaten gravel-walk
were kept separate from the others; and of
these (59 in number) nearly five times as
many had been drawn in by the tip as by
the base; whereas of those extracted from
the lawn and flower-bed, where from the
soil yielding more easily, less care would be
necessary in plugging up the burrows, the
proportion of those drawn in by the tip (130)
to those drawn in by the base (48) was
rather less than three to one.   That these

petioles had been dragged into the burrows for plugging them up, and not for food, was manifest, as neither end, as far as I could see, had been gnawed. As several petioles are used to plug up the same burrow, in one case as many as 10, and in another case as many as 15, the worms may perhaps at first draw in a few by the thicker end so as to save labour; but afterwards a large majority are drawn in by the pointed end, in order to plug up the hole securely.

The fallen petioles of our native ash-tree were next observed, and the rule with most objects, viz., that a large majority are dragged into the burrows by the more pointed end, had not here been followed; and this fact much surprised me at first. These petioles vary in length from 5 to $8\frac{1}{2}$ inches; they are thick and fleshy towards the base, whence they taper gently towards the apex, which is a little enlarged and truncated where the terminal leaflet had been originally attached. Under some ash-trees growing in a grass-field, 229 petioles were pulled out of worm burrows early in January, and of these 51·5 per cent. had been drawn in by the base, and 48·5 per

cent. by the apex. This anomaly was however readily explained as soon as the thick
basal part was examined; for in 78 out of 103
petioles, this part had been gnawed by worms,
just above the horse-shoe shaped articulation.
In most cases there could be no mistake about
the gnawing; for ungnawed petioles which
were examined after being exposed to the
weather for eight additional weeks had not
become more disintegrated or decayed near
the base than elsewhere. It is thus evident
that the thick basal end of the petiole is
drawn in not solely for the sake of plugging
up the mouths of the burrows, but as food.
Even the narrow truncated tips of some
few petioles had been gnawed; and this
was the case in 6 out of 37 which were
examined for this purpose. Worms, after
having drawn in and gnawed the basal end,
often push the petioles out of their burrows;
and then drag in fresh ones, either by
the base for food, or by the apex for plugging up the mouth more effectually. Thus,
out of 37 petioles inserted by their tips,
5 had been previously drawn in by the
base, for this part had been gnawed. Again,

I collected a handful of petioles lying loose
on the ground close to some plugged-up burrows, where the surface was thickly strewed
with other petioles which apparently had
never been touched by worms; and 14 out
of 47 (i.e. nearly one-third), after having
had their bases gnawed had been pushed
out of the burrows and were now lying on
the ground. From these several facts we
may conclude that worms draw in some
petioles of the ash by the base to serve as
food, and others by the tip to plug up the
mouths of their burrows in the most efficient
manner.

The petioles of *Robinia pseudo-acacia* vary
from 4 or 5 to nearly 12 inches in length;
they are thick close to the base before the
softer parts have rotted off, and taper much
towards the upper end. They are so flexible
that I have seen some few doubled up and
thus drawn into the burrows of worms. Un-
fortunately these petioles were not examined
until February, by which time the softer parts
had completely rotted off, so that it was impossible to ascertain whether worms had
gnawed the bases, though this is in itself

probable. Out of 121 petioles extracted from burrows early in February, 68 were embedded by the base, and 53 by the apex. On February 5 all the petioles which had been drawn into the burrows beneath a Robinia, were pulled up; and after an interval of eleven days, 35 petioles had been again dragged in, 19 by the base, and 16 by the apex. Taking these two lots together, 56 per cent. were drawn in by the base, and 44 per cent. by the apex. As all the softer parts had long ago rotted off, we may feel sure, especially in the latter case, that none had been drawn in as food. At this season, therefore, worms drag these petioles into their burrows indifferently by either end, a slight preference being given to the base. This latter fact may be accounted for by the difficulty of plugging up a burrow with objects so extremely thin as are the upper ends. In support of this view, it may be stated that out of the 16 petioles which had been drawn in by their upper ends, the more attenuated terminal portion of 7 had been previously broken off by some accident.

Triangles of paper.—Elongated triangles

were cut out of moderately stiff writing-paper, which was rubbed with raw fat on both sides, so as to prevent their becoming excessively limp when exposed at night to rain and dew. The sides of all the triangles were three inches in length, with the bases of 120 one inch, and of the other 183 half an inch in length. These latter triangles were very narrow or much acuminated.* As a check on the observations presently to be given, similar triangles in a damp state were seized by a very narrow pair of pincers at different points and at all inclinations with reference to the margins, and were then drawn into a short tube of the diameter of a worm-burrow. If seized by the apex, the triangle was drawn straight into the tube, with its margins infolded; if seized at some little distance from the apex, for instance at half an inch, this much was doubled back within the tube. So it was with the base and basal angles, though in this case the triangles offered, as might have been expected, much

---

* In these narrow triangles the apical angle is $9°$ $34'$, and the basal angles $85°$ $13'$. In the broader triangles the apical angle is $19°$ $10'$ and the basal angles $80°$ $25'$.

more resistance to being drawn in. If seized
near the middle the triangle was doubled up,
with the apex and base left sticking out of the
tube. As the sides of the triangles were
three inches in length, the result of their
being drawn into a tube or into a burrow in
different ways, may be conveniently divided
into three groups: those drawn in by the
apex or within an inch of it; those drawn in
by the base or within an inch of it; and those
drawn in by any point in the middle inch.

In order to see how the triangles would be
seized by worms, some in a damp state were
given to worms kept in confinement. They
were seized in three different manners in the
case of both the narrow and broad triangles:
viz., by the margin; by one of the three
angles, which was often completely engulfed
in their mouths; and lastly, by suction applied
to any part of the flat surface. If lines
parallel to the base and an inch apart, are
drawn across a triangle with the sides three
inches in length, it will be divided into three
parts of equal length. Now if worms seized
indifferently by chance any part, they
_ld assuredly seize on the basal part or

division far oftener than on either of the two other divisions. For the area of the basal to the apical part is as 5 to 1, so that the chance of the former being drawn into a burrow by suction, will be as 5 to 1, compared with the apical part. The base offers two angles and the apex only one, so that the former would have twice as good a chance (independently of the size of the angles) of being engulfed in a worm's mouth, as would the apex. It should, however, be stated that the apical angle is not often seized by worms; the margin at a little distance on either side being preferred. I judge of this from having found in 40 out of 46 cases in which triangles had been drawn into burrows by their apical ends, that the tip had been doubled back within the burrow for a length of between $\frac{1}{20}$th of an inch and 1 inch. Lastly, the proportion between the margins of the basal and apical parts is as 3 to 2 for the broad, and $2\frac{1}{2}$ to 2 for the narrow triangles. From these several considerations it might certainly have been expected, supposing that worms seized hold of the triangles by chance, that a considerably larger proportion would have been dragged into the burrows by the basal than by the apical part; but we shall immediately see how different was the result.

Triangles of the above specified sizes were scattered on the ground in many places and on many successive nights near worm-burrows, from which the leaves, petioles, twigs, &c., with which they had been plugged, were removed. Altogether 303 triangles were drawn by worms into their burrows : 12 others were drawn in by both ends, but as it was impossible to judge by which end they had been first seized, these are excluded. Of the 303, 62 per cent. had been drawn in by the apex (using this term for all drawn in by the apical part, one inch in length); 15 per cent. by the middle; and 23 per cent. by the basal part. If they had been drawn indifferently by any point, the proportion for the apical, middle and basal parts would have been 33·3. per cent. for each ; but, as we have just seen, it might have been expected that a much larger proportion would have been drawn in by the basal than by any other part. As the case stands, nearly three times as many were drawn in by the apex as by the base. If we consider the broad triangles by themselves, 59 per cent. were drawn in by the apex, 25 per cent. by the middle, and 16 per cent. by the base.   Of the narrow triangles, 65 per cent. were drawn in by the apex, 14 per cent. by the middle, and 21 per cent. by the base; so that here those drawn in by the apex were more than 3 times as many as those drawn in by the base.   We may therefore conclude that the manner in which the triangles are drawn into the burrows is not a matter of chance.

In eight cases, two triangles had been drawn into the same burrow, and in seven of these cases, one had been drawn in by the apex and the other by the base.   This again indicates that the result is not determined by chance. Worms appear sometimes to revolve in the act of drawing in the triangles, for five out of the whole lot had been wound into an irregular spire round the inside of the burrow.   Worms kept in a warm room drew 63 triangles into their burrows; but, as in the case of the pine-leaves, they worked in a rather careless manner, for only 44 per cent. were drawn in by the apex, 22 per cent. by the middle, and

7

33 per cent. by the base. In five cases, two triangles were drawn into the same burrow.

It may be suggested with much apparent probability that so large a proportion of the triangles were drawn in by the apex, not from the worms having selected this end as the most convenient for the purpose, but from having first tried in other ways and failed. This notion was countenanced by the manner in which worms in confinement were seen to drag about and drop the triangles ; but then they were working carelessly. I did not at first perceive the importance of this subject, but merely noticed that the bases of those triangles which had been drawn in by the apex, were generally clean and not crumpled. The subject was afterwards attended to carefully. In the first place several triangles which had been drawn in by the basal angles, or by the base, or a little above the base, and which were thus much crumpled and dirtied, were left for some hours in water and were then well shaken while immersed ; but neither the dirt nor the creases were thus removed. Only slight creases could be obliterated, even by pulling the wet triangles several

times through my fingers. Owing to the
slime from the worms' bodies, the dirt was
not easily washed off. We may therefore
conclude that if a triangle, before being
dragged in by the apex, had been dragged
into a burrow by its base with even a slight
degree of force, the basal part would long
retain its creases and remain dirty. The condition of 89 triangles (65 narrow and 24
broad ones), which had been drawn in by the
apex, was observed; and the bases of only 7
of them were at all creased, being at the same
time generally dirty. Of the 82 uncreased
triangles, 14 were dirty at the base; but it
does not follow from this fact that these had
first been dragged towards the burrows by
their bases; for the worms sometimes covered
large portions of the triangles with slime,
and these when dragged by the apex over the
ground would be dirtied; and during rainy
weather, the triangles were often dirtied over
one whole side or over both sides. If the
worms had dragged the triangles to the
mouths of their burrows by their bases, as often
as by their apices, and had then perceived,
without actually trying to draw them into the

burrow, that the broader end was not well adapted for this purpose—even in this case a large proportion would probably have had their basal ends dirtied. We may therefore infer—improbable as is the inference—that worms are able by some means to judge which is the best end by which to draw triangles of paper into their burrows.

The per centage results of the foregoing observations on the manner in which worms draw various kinds of objects into the mouths of their burrows may be abridged as follows :—

Nature of Object.	Drawn into the burrows, by or near the apex.	Drawn in, by or near the middle.	Drawn in, by or near the base.
Leaves of various kinds . . .	80	11	9
—— of the Lime, basal margin of blade broad, apex acuminated	79	17	4
—— of a Laburnum, basal part of blade as narrow as, or sometimes little narrower than the apical part. . .	63	10	27
—— of the Rhododendron, basal part of blade often narrower than the apical part . .	34	..	66
—— of Pine-trees, consisting of two needles arising from a common base . . .	..	..	100

Nature of Object.	Drawn into the burrows, by or near the apex.	Drawn in, by or near the middle.	Drawn in, by or near the base.
Petioles of a Clematis, somewhat pointed at the apex, and blunt at the base . .	76	..	24
—— of the Ash, the thick basal end often drawn in to serve as food	48·5	..	51·5
—— of Robinia, extremely thin, especially towards the apex, so as to be ill-fitted for plugging up the burrows .	44	..	56
Triangles of paper, of the two sizes .	62	15	23
—————— of the broad ones alone .	59	25	16
—————— of the narrow ones alone .	65	14	21

If we consider these several cases, we can hardly escape from the conclusion that worms show some degree of intelligence in their manner of plugging up their burrows. Each particular object is seized in too uniform a manner, and from causes which we can generally understand, for the result to be attributed to mere chance. That every object has not been drawn in by its pointed end, may be accounted for by labour having been saved through some being inserted by their broader or thicker ends. No doubt worms are led by instinct to plug up their burrows; and it might have been expected that they would have been led by instinct how best to act in each particular case, independently of intelligence. We see how difficult it is to judge whether intelligence comes into play, for even plants might sometimes be thought to be thus directed; for instance when displaced leaves re-direct their upper surfaces towards the light by extremely complicated movements and by the shortest course. With animals, actions appearing due to intelligence may be performed through inherited habit without any intelligence, although aboriginally thus acquired. Or the habit may have been acquired through the preservation and inheritance of beneficial variations of some other habit; and in this case the new habit will have been acquired independently of intelligence throughout the whole course of its development. There is no à *priori* improbability in worms having acquired special instincts through either of these two latter means. Nevertheless it is incredible that instincts should have been developed in reference to objects, such as the leaves or

petioles of foreign plants, wholly unknown
to the progenitors of the worms which act
in the described manner. Nor are their actions
so unvarying or inevitable as are most true
instincts.

As worms are not guided by special instincts in each particular case, though pos-
sessing a general instinct to plug up their
burrows, and as chance is excluded, the next
most probable conclusion seems to be that
they try in many different ways to draw in
objects, and at last succeed in some one way.
But it is surprising that an animal so low
in the scale as a worm should have the
capacity for acting in this manner, as many
higher animals have no such capacity. For
instance, ants may be seen vainly trying
to drag an object transversely to their
course, which could be easily drawn longitudinally; though after a time they generally act in a wiser manner. M. Fabre
states * that a Sphex—an insect belonging to the same highly-endowed order
with ants—stocks its nest with paralysed

* See his interesting work, 'Souvenirs entomologiques,' 1879,
pp. 168–177.

grasshoppers, which are invariably dragged
into the burrow by their antennæ. When
these were cut off close to the head, the
Sphex seized the palpi; but when these
were likewise cut off, the attempt to drag
its prey into the burrow was given up in
despair. The Sphex had not intelligence
enough to seize one of the six legs or
the ovipositor of the grasshopper, which, as
M. Fabre remarks, would have served equally
well. So again, if the paralysed prey with
an egg attached to it be taken out of the
cell, the Sphex after entering and finding the
cell empty, nevertheless closes it up in the
usual elaborate manner. Bees will try to
escape and go on buzzing for hours on a
window, one half of which has been left open.
Even a pike continued during three months
to dash and bruise itself against the glass
sides of an aquarium, in the vain attempt to
seize minnows on the opposite side.* A cobra-
snake was seen by Mr. Layard † to act much
more wisely than either the pike or the Sphex;

* Möbius, 'Die Bewegungen der Thiere,' &c., 1873, p. 111.
† 'Annals and Mag. of N. History,' series ii. vol. ix. 1852,
p. 338.

it had swallowed a toad lying within a hole, and could not withdraw its head; the toad was disgorged, and began to crawl away; it was again swallowed and again disgorged; and now the snake had learnt by experience, for it seized the toad by one of its legs and drew it out of the hole.   The instincts of even the higher animals are often followed in a senseless or purposeless manner: the weaver-bird will perseveringly wind threads through the bars of its cage, as if building a nest: a squirrel will pat nuts on a wooden floor, as if he had just buried them in the ground: a beaver will cut up logs of wood and drag them about, though there is no water to dam up; and so in many other cases.

Mr. Romanes who has specially studied the minds of animals, believes that we can safely infer intelligence, only when we see an individual profiting by its own experience. By this test the cobra showed some intelligence; but this would have been much plainer if on a second occasion he had drawn a toad out of a hole by its leg.   The Sphex failed signally in this respect.   Now if worms try to drag objects into their burrows first in one way and then in another, until they at last succeed, they profit, at least in each particular instance, by experience.

But evidence has been advanced showing that worms do not habitually try to draw objects into their burrows in many different ways. Thus half-decayed lime-leaves from their flexibility could have been drawn in by their middle or basal parts, and were thus drawn into the burrows in considerable numbers; yet a large majority were drawn in by or near the apex. The petioles of the Clematis could certainly have been drawn in with equal ease by the base and apex; yet three times and in certain cases five times as many were drawn in by the apex as by the base. It might have been thought that the foot-stalks of leaves would have tempted the worms as a convenient handle; yet they are not largely used, except when the base of the blade is narrower than the apex. A large number of the petioles of the ash are drawn in by the base; but this part serves the worms as food. In the case of pine-leaves worms plainly show that they at least do not seize the leaf by chance; but their choice does not appear to be determined by the divergence of the two needles, and the consequent advantage or necessity of drawing them into their burrows by the base. With respect to the triangles of paper, those which had been drawn in by the apex rarely had their bases creased or dirty; and this shows that the worms had not often first tried to drag them in by this end.

If worms are able to judge, either before drawing or after having drawn an object close to the mouths of their burrows, how best to drag it in, they must acquire some notion of its general shape. This they probably acquire by touching it in many places with the anterior extremity of their bodies, which serves as a tactile organ. It may be well to remember how perfect the sense of touch becomes in a man when born blind and deaf, as are worms. If worms have the power of acquiring some notion, however rude, of the shape of an object and of their burrows, as seems to be the case, they deserve to be called intelligent; for they then act in nearly the same manner as would a man under similar circumstances.

To sum up, as chance does not determine the manner in which objects are drawn into the burrows, and as the existence of specialized instincts for each particular case cannot be admitted, the first and most natural supposition is that worms try all methods until they at last succeed; but many appearances are opposed to such a supposition. One alternative alone is left, namely, that worms, although standing low in the scale of organization, possess some degree of intelligence. This will strike every one as very improbable; but it may be doubted whether we know enough about the nervous system of the lower animals to justify our natural distrust of such a conclusion. With respect to the small size of the cerebral ganglia, we should remember what a mass of inherited knowledge, with some power of adapting means to an end, is crowded into the minute brain of a worker-ant.

Means by which worms excavate their burrows.—This is effected in two ways; by pushing away the earth on all sides, and by swallowing it. In the former case, the worm inserts the stretched out and attenuated

anterior extremity of its body into any little
crevice, or hole; and then, as Perrier remarks,* the pharynx is pushed forwards into
this part, which consequently swells and
pushes away the earth on all sides. The
anterior extremity thus serves as a wedge.
It also serves, as we have before seen, for
prehension and suction, and as a tactile organ.
A worm was placed on loose mould, and it
buried itself in between two and three
minutes. On another occasion four worms
disappeared in 15 minutes between the sides
of the pot and the earth, which had been
moderately pressed down. On a third occasion three large worms and a small one
were placed on loose mould well mixed with
fine sand and firmly pressed down, and they
all disappeared, except the tail of one, in
35 minutes. On a fourth occasion six large
worms were placed on argillaceous mud
mixed with sand firmly pressed down, and
they disappeared, except the extreme tips of
the tails of two of them, in 40 minutes. In
none of these cases, did the worms swallow,
as far as could be seen, any earth. They

* 'Archives de Zoolog expér.' tom. iii. 1874, p. 405.

generally entered the ground close to the sides of the pot.

A pot was next filled with very fine ferruginous sand, which was pressed down, well watered, and thus rendered extremely compact. A large worm left on the surface did not succeed in penetrating it for some hours, and did not bury itself completely until 25 hrs. 40 min. had elapsed. This was effected by the sand being swallowed, as was evident by the large quantity ejected from the vent, long before the whole body had disappeared. Castings of a similar nature continued to be ejected from the burrow during the whole of the following day.

As doubts have been expressed by some writers whether worms ever swallow earth solely for the sake of making their burrows, some additional cases may be given. A mass of fine reddish sand, 23 inches in thickness, left on the ground for nearly two years, had been penetrated in many places by worms; and their castings consisted partly of the reddish sand and partly of black earth brought up from beneath the mass. This sand had been dug up from a considerable

depth, and was of so poor a nature that
weeds could not grow on it. It is therefore
highly improbable that it should have been
swallowed by the worms as food. Again in
a field near my house the castings frequently
consist of almost pure chalk, which lies at only
a little depth beneath the surface; and here
again it is very improbable that the chalk
should have been swallowed for the sake of
the very little organic matter which could
have percolated into it from the poor overlying pasture. Lastly, a casting thrown up
through the concrete and decayed mortar
between the tiles, with which the now ruined
aisle of Beaulieu Abbey had formerly been
paved, was washed, so that the coarser
matter alone was left. This consisted of
grains of quartz, micaceous slate, other rocks,
and bricks or tiles, many of them from $\frac{1}{30}$ to
$\frac{1}{10}$ inch in diameter. No one will suppose
that these grains were swallowed as food, yet
they formed more than half of the casting,
for they weighed 19 grains, the whole casting having weighed 33 grains. Whenever a
worm burrows to a depth of some feet in
undisturbed compact ground, it must form its

passage by swallowing the earth ; for it is incredible that the ground could yield on all sides to the pressure of the pharynx when pushed forwards within the worm's body.

That worms swallow a larger quantity of earth for the sake of extracting any nutritious matter which it may contain than for making their burrows, appears to me certain. But as this old belief has been doubted by so high an authority as Claparède, evidence in its favour must be given in some detail. There is no *à priori* improbability in such a belief, for besides other annelids, especially the *Arenicola marina*, which throws up such a profusion of castings on our tidal sands, and which it is believed thus subsists, there are animals belonging to the most distinct classes, which do not burrow, but habitually swallow large quantities of sand ; namely the molluscan Onchidium and many Echinoderms.*

If earth were swallowed only when worms deepened their burrows or made new ones, castings would be thrown up only occasionally ; but in many places fresh castings may

* I state this on the authority of Semper, 'Reisen im Archipel der Philippinen," Th. ii. 1877, p. 30.

be seen every morning, and the amount
of earth ejected from the same burrow on
successive days is large.   Yet worms do not
burrow to a great depth, except when the
weather is very dry or intensely cold.   On
my lawn the black vegetable mould is only
about 5 inches in thickness, and overlies light-
coloured or reddish clayey soil: now when
castings are thrown up in the greatest
profusion, only a small proportion are light
coloured, and it is incredible that the worms
should daily make fresh burrows in every
direction in the thin superficial layer of
dark-coloured humus, unless they obtained
nutriment of some kind from it.   I have
observed a strictly analogous case in a field near
my house where bright red clay lay close
beneath the surface.   Again on one part of
the Downs near Winchester the vegetable
mould overlying the chalk was found to be
only from 3 to 4 inches in thickness; and the
many castings here ejected were as black as
ink and did not effervesce with acids; so that
the worms must have confined themselves to
this thin superficial layer of mould, of which
large quantities were daily swallowed.   In

8

another place at no great distance the castings were white; and why the worms should have burrowed into the chalk in some places and not in others. I am unable to conjecture.

Two great piles of leaves had been left to decay in my grounds, and months after their removal, the bare surface, several yards in diameter, was so thickly covered during several months with castings that they formed an almost continuous layer; and the large number of worms which lived here must have subsisted during these months on nutritious matter contained in the black earth.

The lowest layer from another pile of decayed leaves mixed with some earth was examined under a high power, and the number of spores of various shapes and sizes which it contained was astonishingly great; and these crushed in the gizzards of worms may largely aid in supporting them. Whenever castings are thrown up in the greatest number, few or no leaves are drawn into the burrows; for instance the turf along a hedgerow, about 200 yards in length, was daily observed in the autumn during several weeks, and every morning many fresh castings were seen; but not a single leaf was drawn into these burrows. These castings from their blackness and from the nature of the subsoil could not have been brought up from a greater depth than 6 or 8 inches. On what could these worms have subsisted during this whole time, if not on matter contained in the black earth? On the other hand, whenever a large number of leaves are drawn into the burrows, the worms seem to subsist chiefly on them, for few earth-castings are then ejected on the surface. This difference in the behaviour of worms at different times, perhaps explains a statement by Claparède, namely, that triturated leaves and earth are always found in distinct parts of their intestines.

Worms sometimes abound in places where they can rarely or never obtain dead or living leaves; for instance, beneath the pavement in well-swept courtyards, into which leaves are only occasionally blown. My son Horace examined a house, one corner of which had subsided; and he found here in the cellar, which was extremely damp, many small worm-castings thrown up between the stones with which the cellar was paved; and in this case it is improbable that the worms could ever have obtained leaves.

But the best evidence, known to me, of worms subsisting for at least considerable periods of time solely on the organic matter contained in earth, is afforded by some facts communicated to me by Dr. King. Near Nice large castings abound in extraordinary numbers, so that 5 or 6 were often found within the space of a square foot. They consist of fine, pale-coloured earth, containing calcareous matter, which after having passed through the bodies of worms and being dried, coheres with considerable force. I have reason to believe that these castings had been formed by species of Perichæta, which have been naturalised here from the East.* They

* Dr. King gave me some worms collected near Nice, which, as he believes, had constructed these castings. They were sent to M. Perrier, who with great kindness examined and named them for me: they consisted of *Perichæta affinis,* a native of Cochin China and of the Philippines; *P. Luzonica,* a native of Luzon in the Philippines; and *P. Houlleti,* which lives near Calcutta. M. Perrier informs me that species of Perichæta have been naturalized in the gardens near Montpellier and in Algiers. Before I had any reason to suspect that the tower-like castings from Nice had been formed by worms not endemic in the country, I was

rise like towers (see Fig. 2), with their summits often a little broader than their bases,

Fig. 2

Tower-like casting from near Nice, constructed of earth, voided
probably by a species of Perichæta : of natural size, copied from
a photograph.

sometimes to a height of above 3 and often
to a height of 2½ inches.   The tallest of those

greatly surprised to see how closely they resembled castings sent
to me from near Calcutta, where it is known that species of
Perichæta abound.

which were measured was 3·3 inch in height
and 1 in diameter. A small cylindrical passage runs up the centre of each tower,
through which the worm ascends to eject the
earth which it has swallowed, and thus to
add to its height. A structure of this kind
would not allow leaves being easily dragged
from the surrounding ground into the burrows; and Dr. King, who looked carefully,
never saw even a fragment of a leaf thus
drawn in. Nor could any trace be discovered
of the worms having crawled down the exterior surfaces of the towers in search of
leaves; and had they done so, tracks would
almost certainly have been left on the upper
part whilst it remained soft. It does not,
however, follow that these worms do not
draw leaves into their burrows during some
other season of the year, at which time they
would not build up their towers.

From the several foregoing cases, it can
hardly be doubted that worms swallow earth,
not only for the sake of making their burrows, but for obtaining food. Hensen, however, concludes from his analyses of humus
that worms probably could not live on

ordinary vegetable mould, though he admits
that they might be nourished to some extent
by leaf-mould.* But we have seen that
worms eagerly devour raw meat, fat, and
dead worms; and ordinary mould can hardly
fail to contain many ova, larvæ, and small
living or dead creatures, spores of crypto-
gamic plants, and micrococci, such as those
which give rise to saltpetre. These various
organisms, together with some cellulose from
any leaves and roots not utterly decayed,
might well account for such large quantities
of mould being swallowed by worms. It
may be worth while here to recall the fact
that certain species of Utricularia, which grow
in damp places in the tropics, possess bladders
beautifully constructed for catching minute
subterranean animals; and these traps would
not have been developed unless many small
animals inhabited such soil.

*The depth to which worms penetrate, and
the construction of their burrows.* — Although
worms usually live near the surface, yet they
burrow to a considerable depth during long-

* 'Zeitschrift für wissenschaft. Zoolog.' B. xxviii. 1877
p. 364.

continued dry weather and severe cold. In
Scandinavia, according to Eisen, and in Scotland, according to Mr. Lindsay Carnagie, the
burrows run down to a depth of from 7 to 8
feet; in North Germany, according to Hoffmeister, from 6 to 8 feet, but Hensen says,
from 3 to 6 feet. This latter observer has seen
worms frozen at a depth of $1\frac{1}{2}$ feet beneath
the surface. I have not myself had many
opportunities for observation, but I have often
met with worms at depths of 3 to 4 feet.
In a bed of fine sand overlying the chalk,
which had never been disturbed, a worm was
cut into two at 55 inches, and another was
found here in December at the bottom of its
burrow, at 61 inches beneath the surface.
Lastly, in earth near an old Roman Villa,
which had not been disturbed for many
centuries, a worm was met with at a depth
of 66 inches; and this was in the middle of
August.

The burrows run down perpendicularly, or
more commonly a little obliquely. They are
said sometimes to branch, but as far as I have
seen this does not occur, except in recently
dug ground and near the surface. They are

generally, or as I believe invariably, lined with a thin layer of fine, dark-coloured earth voided by the worms; so that they must at first be made a little wider than their ultimate diameter. I have seen several burrows in undisturbed sand thus lined at a depth of 4 ft. 6 in.; and others close to the surface thus lined in recently dug ground. The walls of fresh burrows are often dotted with little globular pellets of voided earth, still soft and viscid; and these, as it appears, are spread out on all sides by the worm as it travels up or down its burrow. The lining thus formed becomes very compact and smooth when nearly dry, and closely fits the worm's body. The minute reflexed bristles which project in rows on all sides from the body, thus have excellent points of support; and the burrow is rendered well adapted for the rapid movement of the animal. The lining appears also to strengthen the walls, and perhaps saves the worm's body from being scratched. I think so because several burrows which passed through a layer of sifted coal-cinders, spread over turf to a thickness of $1\frac{1}{2}$ inch, had been thus lined to an

unusual thickness.   In this case the worms,
judging from the castings, had pushed the
cinders away on all sides and had not
swallowed any of them.   In another place,
burrows similarly lined, passed through a
layer of coarse coal-cinders, $3\frac{1}{2}$ inches in
thickness.   We thus see that the burrows are
not mere excavations, but may rather be
compared with tunnels lined with cement.

The mouths of the burrow are in addition
often lined with leaves; and this is an instinct
distinct from that of plugging them up, and
does not appear to have been hitherto noticed.
Many leaves of the Scotch-fir or pine (*Pinus
sylvestris*) were given to worms kept in confinement in two pots; and when after several
weeks the earth was carefully broken up, the
upper parts of three oblique burrows were
found surrouuded for lengths of 7, 4, and
$3\frac{1}{2}$ inches with pine-leaves, together with
fragments of other leaves which had been
given the worms as food.   Glass beads and
bits of tile, which had been strewed on the
surface of the soil, were stuck into the interstices between the pine-leaves; and these
interstices were likewise plastered with the

viscid castings voided by the worms. The structures thus formed cohered so well, that I succeeded in removing one with only a little earth adhering to it. It consisted of a slightly curved cylindrical case, the interior of which could be seen through holes in the sides and at either end. The pine-leaves had all been drawn in by their bases; and the sharp points of the needles had been pressed into the lining of voided earth. Had this not been effectually done, the sharp points would have prevented the retreat of the worms into their burrows; and these structures would have resembled traps armed with converging points of wire, rendering the ingress of an animal easy and its egress difficult or impossible. The skill shown by these worms is noteworthy and is the more remarkable, as the Scotch pine is not a native of this district

After having examined these burrows made by worms in confinement, I looked at those in a flower-bed near some Scotch pines. These had all been plugged up in the ordinary manner with the leaves of this tree, drawn in for a length of from 1 to 1½ inch; but the mouths of many of them were likewise lined with them, mingled with fragments of other kinds of leaves, drawn in to a depth of 4 or 5 inches. Worms often remain, as formerly stated, for a long time close to the mouths of their burrows, apparently for warmth; and the basket-like structures formed of leaves would keep their bodies from coming into close contact with the cold damp earth. That they habitually rested on the pine-leaves, was rendered probable by their clean and almost polished surfaces.

The burrows which run far down into the ground, generally, or at least often, terminate in a little enlargement or chamber. Here, according to Hoffmeister, one or several worms pass the winter rolled up into a ball. Mr. Lindsay Carnagie informed me (1838) that he had examined many burrows over a stone-quarry in Scotland, where the overlying boulder-clay and mould had recently been cleared away, and a little vertical cliff thus left. In several cases the same burrow was a little enlarged at two or three points one beneath the other; and all the burrows terminated in a rather large chamber, at a depth of 7 or 8 feet from the surface. These chambers contained many small sharp bits of stone and husks of flax-seeds. They must also have contained living seeds, for on the following spring Mr. Carnagie saw grass-plants sprouting out of some of the intersected chambers. I found at Abinger in Surrey two burrows terminating in similar chambers at a depth of 36 and 41 inches, and these were lined or paved with little pebbles, about as large as mustard seeds; and in one of the chambers there was a decayed oat-grain, with its husk. Hensen likewise states that the bottoms of the burrows are lined with little stones; and where these could not be procured, seeds, apparently of the pear, had been used, as many as fifteen having been carried down into a single burrow, one of which had germinated.[*] We thus see how easily a botanist might be deceived who wished to learn how long deeply buried seeds remained alive, if he were to collect earth from a considerable depth, on the supposition that it could contain only seeds which had long lain buried. It is probable that the little stones,

[*] 'Zeitschrift für wissenschaft. Zoolog.' B. xxviii. 1877, p. 356

as well as the seeds, are carried down from
the surface by being swallowed; for a surprising number of glass beads, bits of tile
and of glass were certainly thus carried down
by worms kept in pots; but some may have
been carried down within their mouths. The
sole conjecture which I can form why worms
line their winter-quarters with little stones
and seeds, is to prevent their closely coiled-up
bodies from coming into close contact with
the surrounding cold soil; and such contact
would perhaps interfere with their respiration
which is effected by the skin alone.

A worm after swallowing earth, whether
for making its burrow or for food, soon comes
to the surface to empty its body. The ejected
earth is thoroughly mingled with the intestinal
secretions, and is thus rendered viscid. After
being dried it sets hard. I have watched
worms during the act of ejection, and when
the earth was in a very liquid state it was
ejected in little spurts, and when not so
liquid by a slow peristaltic movement. It is
not cast indifferently on any side, but with
some care, first on one and then on another
side; the tail being used almost like a trowel.

As soon as a little heap is formed, the worm apparently avoids, for the sake of safety, protruding its tail; and the earthy matter is forced up through the previously deposited soft mass. The mouth of the same burrow is used for this purpose for a considerable time. In the case of the tower-like castings (see Fig. 2) near Nice, and of the similar but still taller towers from Bengal (hereafter to be described and figured) a considerable degree of skill is exhibited in their construction. Dr. King also observed that the passage up these towers hardly ever ran in the same exact line with the underlying burrow, so that a thin cylindrical object such as a haulm of grass, could not be passed down the tower into the burrow; and this change of direction probably serves in some manner as a protection. When a worm comes to the surface to eject earth, the tail protrudes, but when it collects leaves its head must protrude. Worms therefore must have the power of turning round in their closely-fitting burrows; and this, as it appears to us, would be a difficult feat.

Worms do not always eject their castings on

the surface of the ground.   When they can find any cavity, as when burrowing in newly turned-up earth, or between the stems of banked-up plants, they deposit their castings in such places.   So again any hollow beneath a large stone lying on the surface of the ground, is soon filled up with their castings. According to Hensen, old burrows are habitually used for this purpose; but as far as my experience serves, this is not the case, excepting with those near the surface in recently dug ground.   I think that Hensen may have been deceived by the walls of old burrows, lined with black earth, having sunk in or collapsed; for black streaks are thus left, and these are conspicuous when passing through light-coloured soil, and might be mistaken for completely filled-up burrows.

It is certain that old burrows collapse in the course of time; for as we shall see in the next chapter, the fine earth voided by worms, if spread out uniformly, would form in many places in the course of a year a layer $\frac{1}{5}$ of an inch in thickness; so that at any rate this large amount is not deposited within the old unused burrows.   If the burrows did not collapse,

the whole ground would be first thickly
riddled with holes to a depth of about ten
inches, and in fifty years a hollow unsup-
ported space, ten inches in depth, would be
left.   The holes left by the decay of successively formed roots of trees and plants must
likewise collapse in the course of time.

The burrows of worms run down perpendicularly or a little obliquely, and where the
soil is at all argillaceous, there is no difficulty
in believing that the walls would slowly flow
or slide inwards during very wet weather.
When, however, the soil is sandy or
mingled with many small stones, it can
hardly be viscous enough to flow inwards
during even the wettest weather; but another
agency may here come into play.   After
much rain the ground swells, and as it cannot
expand laterally, the surface rises; during
dry weather it sinks again.   For instance, a
large flat stone laid on the surface of a field
sank 3·33 mm. whilst the weather was dry
between May 9th and June 13th, and rose
1·91 mm. between September 7th and 19th,
much rain having fallen during the latter
part of this time.   During frosts and thaws

9

the movements were twice as great. These observations were made by my son Horace, who will hereafter publish an account of the movements of this stone during successive wet and dry seasons, and of the effects of its being undermined by worms. Now when the ground swells, if it be penetrated by cylindrical holes, such as worm-burrows, their walls will tend to yield and be pressed inwards; and the yielding will be greater in the deeper parts (supposing the whole to be equally moistened) from the greater weight of the superincumbent soil which has to be raised, than in the parts near the surface. When the ground dries, the walls will shrink a little and the burrows will be a little enlarged. Their enlargement, however, through the lateral contraction of the ground, will not be favoured, but rather opposed, by the weight of the superincumbent soil.

Distribution of Worms.—Earth-worms are found in all parts of the world, and some of the genera have an enormous range.* They inhabit the most isolated islands; they

* Perrier, 'Archives de Zoolog. expér.' tom. 3, p. 378, 1874.

abound in Iceland, and are known to exist in the West Indies, St. Helena, Madagascar, New Caledonia and Tahiti. In the Antarctic regions, worms from Kerguelen Land have been described by Ray Lankester; and I found them in the Falkland Islands. How they reach such isolated islands is at present quite unknown. They are easily killed by salt-water, and it does not appear probable that young worms or their egg-capsules could be carried in earth adhering to the feet or beaks of land-birds. Moreover Kerguelen Land is not now inhabited by any land-bird.

In this volume we are chiefly concerned with the earth cast up by worms, and I have gleaned a few facts on this subject with respect to distant lands. Worms throw up plenty of castings in the United States. In Venezuela, castings, probably ejected by species of Urochæta, are common in the gardens and fields, but not in the forests, as I hear from Dr. Ernst of Caracas. He collected 156 castings from the court-yard of his house, having an area of 200 square yards. They varied in bulk from half a cubic centimeter to five cubic centimeters, and were on an average

three cubic centimeters. They were, therefore
of small size in comparison with those often
found in England; for six large castings from
a field near my house averaged 16 cubic centimeters. Several species of earth-worms are
common in St. Catharina in South Brazil, and
Fritz Müller informs me " that in most parts of
" the forests and pasture-lands, the whole soil,
" to a depth of a quarter of a metre, looks as if it
" had passed repeatedly through the intestines
" of earth-worms, even where hardly any cast-
" ings are to be seen on the surface."   A
gigantic but very rare species is found there,
the burrows of which are sometimes even two
centimeters or nearly $\frac{4}{5}$ of an inch in diameter,
and which apparently penetrate the ground
to a great depth.

In the dry climate of New South Wales, I
hardly expected that worms would be common; but Dr. G. Krefft of Sydney, to whom
I applied, after making enquiries from
gardeners and others, and from his own
observations, informs me that their castings
abound. He sent me some collected after
heavy rain, and they consisted of little pellets,
about ·15 inch in diameter; and the blackened

sandy earth of which they were formed still cohered with considerable tenacity.

The late Mr. John Scott of the Botanic Gardens near Calcutta made many observations for me on worms living under the hot and humid climate of Bengal. The castings abound almost everywhere, in jungles and in the open ground, to a greater degree, as he thinks, than in England. After the water has subsided from the flooded rice-fields, the whole surface very soon becomes studded with castings—a fact which much surprised Mr. Scott, as he did not know how long worms could survive beneath water. They cause much trouble in the Botanic garden, "for "some of the finest of our lawns can be kept "in anything like order only by being almost "daily rolled; if left undisturbed for a few days "they become studded with large castings." These closely resemble those described as abounding near Nice; and they are probably the work of a species of Perichæta. They stand up like towers, with an open passage in the centre.

A figure of one of these castings from a photograph is here given (Fig. 3). The

largest received by me was $3\frac{1}{2}$ inches in
height and 1·35 inch in diameter; another

Fig. 3.

A tower-like casting, probably ejected by a species of Perichæta,
from the Botanic Garden, Calcutta : of natural size, engraved
from a photograph.

was only $\frac{3}{4}$ inch in diameter and $2\frac{3}{4}$ in height.

In the following year, Mr. Scott measured several of the largest; one was 6 inches in height and nearly $1\frac{1}{2}$ in diameter : two others were 5 inches in height and respectively 2 and rather more than $2\frac{1}{2}$ inches in diameter. The average weight of the 22 castings sent to me was 35 grammes ($1\frac{1}{4}$ oz.); and one of them weighed 44·8 grammes (or 2 oz.).   All these castings were thrown up either in one night or in two.   Where the ground in Bengal is dry, as under large trees, castings of a different kind are found in vast numbers : these consist of little oval or conical bodies, from about the $\frac{1}{30}$ to rather above $\frac{1}{10}$ of an inch in length.   They are obviously voided by a distinct species of worms.

The period during which worms neai Calcutta display such extraordinary activity lasts for only a little over two months, namely, during the cool season after the rains. At this time they are generally found within about 10 inches beneath the surface.   During the hot season they burrow to a greater depth, and are then found coiled up and apparently hybernating.   Mr. Scott has never seen them at a greater depth than $2\frac{1}{2}$ feet, but has heard of their having been found at 4 feet. Within the forests, fresh castings may be found even during the hot season. The worms in the Botanic garden, during the cool and dry season, draw many leaves and little sticks into the mouths of their burrows, like our English worms; but they rarely act in this manner during the rainy season.

Mr. Scott saw worm-castings on the lofty mountains of Sikkim in North India. In South India Dr. King found in one place, on the plateau of the Nilgiris, at an elevation of 7000 feet, "a good many castings," which are interesting for their great size. The worms which eject them are seen only during the wet season, and are reported to be from 12 to 15 inches in length, and as thick as a man's little finger. These castings were collected by Dr. King after a period of 110 days without any rain; and they must have been ejected either during the north-east or more probably during the previous south-west monsoon; for their surfaces had suffered some disintegration and they were penetrated by many fine roots. A drawing is here given (Fig. 4) of one which

seems to have best retained its original size
and appearance.   Notwithstanding some loss
from disintegration, five of the largest of these
castings (after having been well sun-dried)
weighed each on an average 89·5 grammes,

Fig. 4.

A casting from the Nilgiri Mountains in South India; of
natural size, engraved from a photograph.

or above   3 oz.; and the largest weighed
123·14 grammes, or 4⅓ oz.,—that is above a
quarter of a pound! The largest convolutions
were rather more than one inch in diameter;
but it is probable that they had subsided a little

whilst soft, and that their diameters had thus
been increased. Some had flowed so much
that they now consisted of a pile of almost flat
confluent cakes. All were formed of fine,
rather light-coloured earth, and were surprisingly hard and compact, owing no doubt to
the animal matter by which the particles of
earth had been cemented together. They
did not disintegrate, even when left for some
hours in water. Although they had been
cast up on the surface of gravelly soil, they
contained extremely few bits of rock, the
largest of which was only ·15 inch in
diameter.

Dr. King saw in Ceylon a worm about 2
feet in length and ½ inch in diameter; and
he was told that it was a very common species
during the wet season. These worms must
throw up castings at least as large as those on
the Nilgiri Mountains; but Dr. King saw
none during his short visit to Ceylon. Sufficient facts have now been given, showing
that worms do much work in bringing up
fine earth to the surface in most or all parts
of the world, and under the most different
climates.

CHAPTER III.

THE AMOUNT OF FINE EARTH BROUGHT UP BY WORMS TO THE SURFACE.

Rate at which various objects strewed on the surface of grass-fields are covered up by the castings of worms—The burial of a paved path—The slow subsidence of great stones left on the surface—The number of worms which live within a given space—The weight of earth ejected from a burrow, and from all the burrows within a given space—The thickness of the layer of mould which the castings on a given space would form within a given time if uniformly spread out—The slow rate at which mould can increase to a great thickness—Conclusion.

WE now come to the more immediate subject of this volume, namely the amount of earth which is brought up by worms from beneath the surface, and is afterwards spread out more or less completely by the rain and wind. The amount can be judged of by two methods,—by the rate at which objects left on the surface are buried, and more accurately by weighing the quantity brought up within a given time. We will begin with the first method, as it was first followed.

Near Maer Hall in Staffordshire, quick-lime had been spread about the year 1827 thickly over a field of good pasture-land, which had not since been ploughed. Some square holes were dug in this field in the beginning of October 1837; and the sections showed a layer of turf, formed by the matted roots of the grasses, $\frac{1}{2}$ inch in thickness, beneath which, at a depth of $2\frac{1}{2}$ inches (or 3 inches from the surface), a layer of the lime in powder or in small lumps could be distinctly seen running all round the vertical sides of the holes. The soil beneath the layer of lime was either gravelly or of a coarse sandy nature, and differed considerably in appearance from the overlying dark-coloured fine mould. Coal-cinders had been spread over a part of this same field either in the year 1833 or 1834; and when the above holes were dug, that is after an interval of 3 or 4 years, the cinders formed a line of black spots round the holes, at a depth of 1 inch beneath the surface, parallel to and above the white layer of lime. Over another part of this field

cinders had been strewed, only about half-a-
year before, and these either still lay on the
surface or were entangled among the roots of
the grasses; and I here saw the commencement of the burying process, for worm-castings had been heaped on several of the
smaller fragments.   After an interval of
$4\frac{3}{4}$ years this field was re-examined, and now
the two layers of lime and cinders were found
almost everywhere at a greater depth than
before by nearly 1 inch, we will say by $\frac{3}{4}$ of
an inch.   Therefore mould to an average
thickness of ·22 of an inch had been annually
brought up by the worms, and had been
spread over the surface of this field.

Coal-cinders had been strewed over another
field, at a date which could not be positively
ascertained, so thickly that they formed
(October, 1837) a layer, 1 inch in thickness
at a depth of about 3 inches from the surface.
The layer was so continuous that the overlying dark vegetable mould was connected
with the sub-soil of red clay only by the roots
of the grasses; and when these were broken,
the mould and the red clay fell apart.   In a
third field, on which coal-cinders and burnt

marl had been strewed several times at unknown dates, holes were dug in 1842; and a
layer of cinders could be traced at a depth
of $3\frac{1}{2}$ inches, beneath which at a depth of
$9\frac{1}{2}$ inches from the surface there was a line
of cinders together with burnt marl. On the
sides of one hole there were two layers of
cinders, at 2 and $3\frac{1}{2}$ inches beneath the surface; and below them at a depth in parts
of $9\frac{1}{2}$, and in other parts of $10\frac{1}{2}$ inches there
were fragments of burnt marl. In a fourth
field two layers of lime, one above the other,
could be distinctly traced, and beneath them
a layer of cinders and burnt marl at a depth
of from 10 to 12 inches below the surface.

A piece of waste, swampy land was
enclosed, drained, ploughed, harrowed and
thickly covered in the year 1822 with burnt
marl and cinders. It was sowed with grass
seeds, and now supports a tolerably good but
coarse pasture. Holes were dug in this field
in 1837, or 15 years after its reclamation,
and we see in the accompanying diagram
(Fig. 5), reduced to half of the natural scale,
that the turf was $\frac{1}{2}$ inch thick, beneath which
there was a layer of vegetable mould $2\frac{1}{2}$ inches

thick.   This layer did not contain fragments
of any kind ; but beneath it there was a layer
of mould, 1½ inch in thickness, full of fragments

Fig. 5.

Section, reduced to half the natural scale, of the vegetable mould
  in a field, drained and reclaimed fifteen years previously; A,
  turf; B, vegetable mould without any stones; C, mould with
  fragments of burnt marl, coal-cinders and quartz pebbles;
  D, sub-soil of black, peaty sand with quartz pebbles.

of burnt marl, conspicuous from their red
colour, one of which near the bottom was an

inch in length; and other fragments of coal-
cinders together with a few white quartz
pebbles. Beneath this layer and at a depth of
4½ inches from the surface, the original black,
peaty, sandy soil with a few quartz pebbles
was encountered. Here therefore the fragments of burnt marl and cinders had been
covered in the course of 15 years by a layer
of fine vegetable mould, only 2½ inches in
thickness, excluding the turf. Six and a half
years subsequently this field was re-examined,
and the fragments were now found at from
4 to 5 inches beneath the surface. So that
in this interval of 6½ years, about 1½ inch of
mould had been added to the superficial layer.
I am surprised that a greater quantity had
not been brought up during the whole 21½
years, for in the closely underlying black,
peaty soil there were many worms. It is,
however, probable that formerly, whilst the
land remained poor, worms were scanty; and
the mould would then have accumulated
slowly. The average annual increase of thickness for the whole period is ·19 of an inch.

Two other cases are worth recording. In
the spring of 1835, a field, which had

long existed as poor pasture and was so
swampy that it trembled slightly when
stamped on, was thickly covered with red
sand so that the whole surface appeared at
first bright red.   When holes were dug in
this field after an interval of about $2\frac{1}{2}$ years,
the sand formed a layer at a depth of $\frac{3}{4}$ in.
beneath the surface.   In 1842 (i.e., 7 years
after the sand had been laid on) fresh holes
were dug, and now the red sand formed a
distinct layer, 2 inches beneath the surface,
or $1\frac{1}{2}$ inch beneath the turf; so that on an
average, ·21 inches of mould had been annually brought to the surface.   Immediately
beneath the layer of red sand, the original
substratum of black sandy peat extended.

A grass field, likewise not far from Maer
Hall, had formerly been thickly covered with
marl, and was then left for several years as
pasture; it was afterwards ploughed.   A
friend had three trenches dug in this field
28 years after the application of the marl,*

* This case is given in a postscript to my paper in the
'Transact. Geolog. Soc.' (Vol. v. p. 505), and contains a serious
error, as in the account received I mistook the figure 30 for 80.
The tenant, moreover, formerly said that he had marled the field
thirty years before, but was now positive that this was done in

10

and a layer of the marl fragments could be traced at a depth, carefully measured, of 12 inches in some parts, and of 14 inches in other parts. This difference in depth depended on the layer being horizontal, whilst the surface consisted of ridges and furrows from the field having been ploughed. The tenant assured me that it had never been turned up to a greater depth than from 6 to 8 inches; and as the fragments formed an unbroken horizontal layer from 12 to 14 inches beneath the surface, these must have been buried by the worms whilst the land was in pasture before it was ploughed, for otherwise they would have been indiscriminately scattered by the plough throughout the whole thickness of the soil. Four-and-a-half years afterwards I had three holes dug in this field, in which potatoes had been lately planted, and the layer of marl-fragments was now found 13 inches beneath the bottoms of the furrows, and therefore probably 15 inches

---

1809, that is twenty-eight years before the first examination of the field by my friend. The error, as far as the figure 80 is concerned, was corrected in an article by me, in the 'Gardeners Chronicle,' 1844, p. 218.

beneath the general level of the field. It should, however, be observed that the thickness of the blackish sandy soil, which had been thrown up by the worms above the marl-fragments in the course of 32½ years, would have measured less than 15 inches, if the field had always remained as pasture, for the soil would in this case have been much more compact. The fragments of marl almost rested on an undisturbed sub-stratum of white sand with quartz pebbles; and as this would be little attractive to worms, the mould would hereafter be very slowly increased by their action.

We will now give some cases of the action of worms, on land differing widely from the dry sandy or the swampy pastures just described. The chalk formation extends all round my house in Kent; and its surface, from having been exposed during an immense period to the dissolving action of rain-water, is extremely irregular, being abruptly festooned and penetrated by many deep well-like cavities.* During the dissolution of the

---

* These pits or pipes are still in process of formation. During the last forty years I have seen or heard of five cases, in which a

chalk, the insoluble matter, including a vast
number of unrolled flints of all sizes, has

---

circular space, several feet in diameter, suddenly fell in, leaving
on the field an open hole with perpendicular sides, some feet in
depth. This occurred in one of my own fields, whilst it was
being rolled, and the hinder quarters of the shaft horse fell in; two
or three cart-loads of rubbish were required to fill up the hole.
The subsidence occurred where there was a broad depression, as
if the surface had fallen in at several former periods. I heard
of a hole which must have been suddenly formed at the bottom
of a small shallow pool, where sheep had been washed during
many years, and into which a man thus occupied fell to his great
terror. The rain-water over this whole district sinks perpendicularly into the ground, but the chalk is more porous in certain
places than in others. Thus the drainage from the overlying
clay is directed to certain points, where a greater amount of calcareous matter is dissolved than elsewhere. Even narrow open
channels are sometimes formed in the solid chalk. As the chalk
is slowly dissolved over the whole country, but more in some
parts than in others, the undissolved residue—that is the overlying mass of red clay with flints,—likewise sinks slowly down,
and tends to fill up the pipes or cavities. But the upper part
of the red clay holds together, aided probably by the roots of
plants, for a longer time than the lower parts, and thus forms
a roof, which sooner or later falls in, as in the above mentioned
five cases. The downward movement of the clay may be compared with that of a glacier, but is incomparably slower; and this
movement accounts for a singular fact, namely that the much
elongated flints which are embedded in the chalk in a nearly
horizontal position, are commonly found standing nearly or quite
upright in the red clay. This fact is so common that the workmen assured me that this was their natural position. I roughly
measured one which stood vertically, and it was of the same
length and of the same relative thickness as one of my arms
These elongated flints must get placed in their upright position,

been left on the surface and forms a bed of
stiff red clay, full of flints, and generally
from 6 to 14 feet in thickness. Over the red
clay, wherever the land has long remained as
pasture, there is a layer a few inches in
thickness, of dark-coloured vegetable mould.

A quantity of broken chalk was spread,
on December 20, 1842, over a part of a field
near my house, which had existed as pasture
certainly for 30, probably for twice or thrice
as many years. The chalk was laid on the
land for the sake of observing at some future
period to what depth it would become buried.
At the end of November, 1871, that is after an
interval of 29 years, a trench was dug across
this part of the field; and a line of white nodules
could be traced on both sides of the trench, at
a depth of 7 inches from the surface. The
mould, therefore, (excluding the turf) had

on the same principle that a trunk of a tree left on a glacier
assumes a position parallel to the line of motion. The flints
in the clay which form almost half its bulk, are very often
broken, though not rolled or abraded; and this may be accounted for by their mutual pressure, whilst the whole mass is
subsiding. I may add that the chalk here appears to have been
originally covered in parts by a thin bed of fine sand with some
perfectly rounded flint pebbles, probably of Tertiary age; for such
sand often partly fills up the deeper pits or cavities in the chalk

here been thrown up at an average rate of ·22 inches per year. Beneath the line of chalk nodules there was in parts hardly any fine earth free of flints, while in other parts there was a layer, 2¼ inches in thickness. In this latter case the mould was altogether 9¼ inches thick; and in one such spot a nodule of chalk and a smooth flint pebble, both of which must have been left at some former time on the surface, were found at this depth. At from 11 to 12 inches beneath the surface, the undisturbed reddish clay, full of flints, extended. The appearance of the above nodules of chalk surprised me much at first, as they closely resembled water-worn pebbles, whereas the freshly-broken fragments had been angular. But on examining the nodules with a lens, they no longer appeared water-worn, for their surfaces were pitted through unequal corrosion, and minute, sharp points, formed of broken fossil shells, projected from them. It was evident that the corners of the original fragments of chalk had been wholly dissolved, from presenting a large surface to the carbonic acid dissolved in the rain-water and to that gener·

ated in soil containing vegetable matter, as well as to the humus-acids.[*] The projecting corners would also, relatively to the other parts, have been embraced by a larger number of living rootlets; and these have the power of even attacking marble, as Sachs has shown. Thus, in the course of 29 years, buried angular fragments of chalk had been converted into well-rounded nodules.

Another part of this same field was mossy, and as it was thought that sifted coal-cinders would improve the pasture, a thick layer was spread over this part either in 1842 or 1843 and another layer some years afterwards. In 1871 a trench was here dug, and many cinders lay in a line at a depth of 7 inches beneath the surface, with another line at a depth of $5\frac{1}{2}$ inches parallel to the one beneath. In another part of this field, which had formerly existed as a separate one, and which it was believed had been pasture-land for more than a century, trenches were dug to see how thick the vegetable mould was. By chance the first trench was made at a spot where at some former period,

[*] S. W. Johnson, 'How Crops Feed,' 1870, p. 139

certainly more than forty years before, a
large hole had been filled up with coarse red
clay, flints, fragments of chalk, and gravel;
and here the fine vegetable mould was only
from $4\frac{1}{8}$ to $4\frac{3}{8}$ inches in thickness. In
another and undisturbed place, the mould
varied much in thickness, namely from $6\frac{1}{2}$
to $8\frac{1}{2}$ inches; beneath which a few small
fragments of brick were found in one
place. From these several cases, it would
appear that during the last 29 years mould
has been heaped on the surface at an
average annual rate of from ·2 to ·22 of an
inch. But in this district when a ploughed
field is first laid down in grass, the mould
accumulates at a much slower rate. The
rate, also, must become very much slower
after a bed of mould, several inches in thickness, has been formed; for the worms then
live chiefly near the surface, and burrow
down to a greater depth so as to bring up
fresh earth from below, only during the
winter when the weather is very cold (at
which time worms were found in this field at
a depth of 26 inches) and during summer
when the weather is very dry.

A field, which adjoins the one just described, slopes in one part rather steeply
(viz., at from 10° to 15°); this part was last
ploughed in 1841, was then harrowed and
left to become pasture-land. For several
years it was clothed with an extremely scant
vegetation, and was so thickly covered with
small and large flints (some of them half as
large as a child's head) that the field was
always called by my sons "the stony field."
When they ran down the slope the stones
clattered together. I remember doubting
whether I should live to see these larger flints
covered with vegetable mould and turf. But
the smaller stones disappeared before many
years had elapsed, as did every one of the
larger ones after a time; so that after thirty
years (1871) a horse could gallop over the
compact turf from one end of the field to the
other, and not strike a single stone with his
shoes. To anyone who remembered the
appearance of the field in 1842, the transformation was wonderful. This was certainly
the work of the worms, for though castings
were not frequent for several years, yet some
were thrown up month after month, and

these gradually increased in numbers as the pasture improved. In the year 1871 a trench was dug on the above slope, and the blades of grass were cut off close to the roots, so that the thickness of the turf and of the vegetable mould could be measured accurately. The turf was rather less than half an inch, and the mould, which did not contain any stones, $2\frac{1}{2}$ inches in thickness. Beneath this lay coarse clayey earth full of flints, like that in any of the neighbouring ploughed fields. This coarse earth easily fell apart from the overlying mould when a spit was lifted up. The average rate of accumulation of the mould during the whole thirty years was only ·083 inch per year (i.e., nearly one inch in twelve years); but the rate must have been much slower at first, and afterwards considerably quicker.

The transformation in the appearance of this field, which had been effected beneath my eyes, was afterwards rendered the more striking, when I examined in Knole Park a dense forest of lofty beech-trees, beneath which nothing grew. Here the ground was thickly strewed with large naked stones, and worm-castings were almost wholly absent. Obscure lines and irregularities on the surface indicated that the land had been cultivated some centuries ago. It is probable that a thick wood of young beech-trees sprung up so quickly, that time enough was not allowed for worms to cover up the stones with their castings, before the site became unfitted for their existence. Anyhow the contrast between the state of the now miscalled " stony field," well stocked with worms, and the present state of the ground beneath the old beech-trees in Knole Park, where worms appeared to be absent, was striking.

A narrow path running across part of my lawn was paved in 1843 with small flag-stones, set edgeways; but worms threw up many castings and weeds grew thickly between them. During several years the path was weeded and swept; but ultimately the weeds and worms prevailed, and the gardener ceased to sweep, merely mowing off the weeds, as often as the lawn was mowed. The path soon became almost covered up, and after several years no trace of it was left. On removing, in 1877, the thin overlying layer of turf, the small flag-stones, all in their proper places, were found covered by an inch of fine mould.

Two recently published accounts of substances strewed on the surface of pasture-land, having become buried through the action of worms, may be here noticed. The Rev. H. C. Key had a ditch cut in a field, over which coal-ashes had been spread, as it was believed, eighteen years before; and on the clean-cut perpendicular sides of the ditch, at a depth of at least seven inches, there could be seen, for a length of 60 yards, " a distinct, very " even, narrow line of coal-ashes, mixed with " small coal, perfectly parallel with the top-sward."* This parallelism and the length of the section gives interest to the case. Secondly, Mr. Dancer states† that crushed bones had been thickly strewed over a field; and " some years " afterwards " these were found "several inches " below the surface, at a uniform depth." Worms appear to act in the same manner in New Zealand as in Europe; for Professor J.

* 'Nature,' November 1877, p. 28.
† 'Proc. Phil. Soc.' of Manchester, 1877, p. 247.

von Haast has described * a section near the coast, consisting of mica-schist, " covered by " 5 or 6 feet of loess, above which about 12 " inches of vegetable soil had accumulated." Between the loess and the mould there was a layer from 3 to 6 inches in thickness, consisting of "cores, implements, flakes, and " chips, all manufactured from hard basaltic " rock." It is therefore probable that the aborigines, at some former period, had left these objects on the surface, and that they had afterwards been slowly covered up by the castings of worms.

Farmers in England are well aware that objects of all kinds, left on the surface of pasture-land, after a time disappear, or, as they say, work themselves downwards. How powdered lime, cinders, and heavy stones, can work down, and at the same rate, through the matted roots of a grass-covered surface, is a question which has probably never occurred to them.†

* 'Trans. of the New Zealand Institute,' vol. xii., 1880, p. 152.
† Mr. Lindsay Carnagie, in a letter (June 1838) to Sir C. Lyell, remarks that Scotch farmers are afraid of putting lime on ploughed land until just before it is laid down for pasture, from a belief that it has some tendency to sink. He adds: "Some

The Sinking of great Stones through the Action of Worms.—When a stone of large size and of irregular shape is left on the surface of the ground, it rests, of course, on the more protuberant parts; but worms soon fill up with their castings all the hollow spaces on the lower side; for, as Hensen remarks, they like the shelter of stones. As soon as the hollows are filled up, the worms eject the earth which they have swallowed beyond the circumference of the stones; and thus the surface of the ground is raised all round the stone. As the burrows excavated directly beneath the stone after a time collapse, the stone sinks a little.* Hence it is, that boulders which at some ancient

---

years since, in autumn, I laid lime on an oat-stubble and ploughed it down; thus bringing it into immediate contact with the dead vegetable matter, and securing its thorough mixture through the means of all the subsequent operations of fallow. In consequence of the above prejudice, I was considered to have committed a great fault; but the result was eminently successful, and the practice was *partially* followed. By means of Mr. Darwin's observations, I think the prejudice will be removed."

* This conclusion, which, as we shall immediately see, is fully justified. It is of some little importance, as the so-called bench-stones, which surveyors fix in the ground as a record of their levels, will thus become false standards. My son Horace intends at some future period to ascertain how far this has occurred.

period have rolled down from a rocky mountain or cliff on to a meadow at its base, are
always somewhat embedded in the soil; and,
when removed, leave an exact impression of
their lower surfaces in the under-lying fine
mould.   If, however, a boulder is of such
huge dimensions, that the earth beneath is
kept dry, such earth will not be inhabited
by worms, and the boulder will not sink
into the ground.

A lime-kiln formerly stood in a grass-field
near Leith Hill Place in Surrey, and was
pulled down 35 years before my visit;
all the loose rubbish had been carted away,
excepting three large stones of quartzose
sandstone, which it was thought might hereafter be of some use.   An old workman remembered that they had been left on a bare
surface of broken bricks and mortar, close to
the foundations of the kiln; but the whole
surrounding surface is now covered with turf
and mould.   The two largest of these stones
had never since been moved; nor could this
easily have been done, as, when I had them
removed, it was the work of two men with
levers.   One of these stones, and not the

largest, was 64 inches long, 17 inches broad,
and from 9 to 10 inches in thickness.   Its
lower surface was somewhat protuberant in
the middle; and this part still rested on
broken bricks and mortar, showing the truth
of the old workman's account.   Beneath the
brick rubbish the natural sandy soil, full of
fragments of sandstone was found; and this
could have yielded very little, if at all, to
the weight of the stone, as might have been
expected if the sub-soil had been clay.   The
surface of the field, for a distance of about
9 inches round the stone, gradually sloped up
to it, and close to the stone stood in most
places about 4 inches above the surrounding
ground.   The base of the stone was buried
from 1 to 2 inches beneath the general level,
and the upper surface projected about 8
inches above this level, or about 4 inches
above the sloping border of turf.   After the
removal of the stone it became evident that
one of its pointed ends must at first have
stood clear above the ground by some inches,
but its upper surface was now on a level
with the surrounding turf.   When the stone
was removed, an exact cast of its lower

side, forming a shallow crateriform hollow,
was left, the inner surface of which consisted
of fine black mould, excepting where the
more protuberant parts rested on the brick-
rubbish.   A transverse section of this stone,
together with its bed, drawn from measurements made after it had been displaced, is
here given on a scale of $\frac{1}{2}$ inch to a foot
(Fig. 6).   The turf-covered border which

Fig. 6.

Transverse section across a large stone, which had lain on a
grass-field for 35 years. A A, general level of the field. The
underlying brick rubbish has not been represented. Scale
$\frac{1}{2}$ inch to one foot.

sloped up to the stone, consisted of fine
vegetable mould, in one part 7 inches in
thickness. This evidently consisted of worm-
castings, several of which had been recently
ejected. The whole stone had sunk in the
thirty-five years, as far as I could judge,
about 1$\frac{1}{2}$ inch; and this must have been due

to the brick-rubbish beneath the more protuberant parts having been undermined by
worms. At this rate the upper surface of the
stone, if it had been left undisturbed, would
have sunk to the general level of the field
in 247 years; but before this could have
occurred, some earth would have been washed
down by heavy rain from the castings on the
raised border of turf over the upper surface
of the stone.

The second stone was larger than the one
just described, viz., 67 inches in length, 39 in
breadth, and 15 in thickness. The lower
surface was nearly flat, so that the worms
must soon have been compelled to eject their
castings beyond its circumference. The stone
as a whole had sunk about 2 inches into the
ground. At this rate it would have required
262 years for its upper surface to have sunk
to the general level of the field. The up-
wardly sloping, turf-covered border round
the stone was broader than in the last case,
viz., from 14 to 16 inches; and why this
should be so, I could see no reason. In most
parts this border was not so high as in the
last case, viz., from 2 to 2½ inches, but in one

place it was as much as 5½. Its average
height close to the stone was probably about
3 inches, and it thinned out to nothing. If
so, a layer of fine earth, 15 inches in breadth
and 1½ inch in average thickness, of sufficient
length to surround the whole of the much
elongated slab, must have been brought up
by the worms in chief part from beneath the
stone in the course of 35 years. This
amount would be amply sufficient to account
for its having sunk about 2 inches into the
ground; more especially if we bear in mind
that a good deal of the finest earth would
have been washed by heavy rain from the
castings ejected on the sloping border down
to the level of the field. Some fresh castings
were seen close to the stone. Nevertheless,
on digging a large hole to a depth of 18
inches where the stone had lain, only two
worms and a few burrows were seen, although
the soil was damp and seemed favourable for
worms. There were some large colonies of
ants beneath the stone, and possibly since
their establishment the worms had decreased
in number.

The third stone was only about half as

large as the others; and two strong boys could together have rolled it over. I have no doubt that it had been rolled over at a moderately recent time, for it now lay at some distance from the two other stones at the bottom of a little adjoining slope. It rested also on fine earth, instead of partly on brick-rubbish. In agreement with this conclusion, the raised surrounding border of turf was only 1 inch high in some parts, and 2 inches in other parts. There were no colonies of ants beneath this stone, and on digging a hole where it had lain, several burrows and worms were found.

At Stonehenge, some of the outer Druidical stones are now prostrate, having fallen at a remote but unknown period; and these have become buried to a moderate depth in the ground. They are surrounded by sloping borders of turf, on which recent castings were seen. Close to one of these fallen stones, which was 17 ft. long, 6 ft. broad, and $28\frac{1}{2}$ inches thick, a hole was dug; and here the vegetable mould was at least $9\frac{1}{2}$ inches in thickness. At this depth a flint was found, and a little higher up on one side of the hole a fragment of glass.   The base of the stone lay about $9\frac{1}{2}$ inches beneath the level of the surrounding ground, and its upper surface 19 inches above the ground.

A hole was also dug close to a second huge stone, which in falling had broken into two pieces; and this must have happened long ago, judging from the weathered aspect of the fractured ends.   The base was buried to a depth of 10 inches, as was ascertained by driving an iron skewer horizontally into the ground beneath it.   The vegetable mould forming the turf-covered sloping border round the stone, on which many castings had recently been ejected, was 10 inches in thickness; and most of this mould must have been brought up by worms from beneath its base. At a distance of 8 yards from the stone, the mould was only $5\frac{1}{2}$ inches in thickness (with a piece of tobacco pipe at a depth of 4 inches), and this rested on broken flint and chalk which could not have easily yielded to the pressure or weight of the stone.

A straight rod was fixed horizontally (by the aid of a spirit-level) across a third fallen stone, which was 7 feet 9 inches long; and the

contour of the projecting parts and of the adjoining ground, which was not quite level,
was thus ascertained, as shown in the accompanying diagram (Fig. 7) on a scale of

Fig. 7.

Section through one of the fallen Druidical stones at Stonehenge,
showing how much it had sunk into the ground.   Scale ½ inch
to 1 foot.

½ inch to a foot.   The turf-covered border
sloped up to the stone on one side to a
height of 4 inches, and on the opposite side
to only 2½ inches above the general level.
A hole was dug on the eastern side, and the
base of the stone was here found to lie at a
depth of 4 inches beneath the general level
of the ground, and of 8 inches beneath the
top of the sloping turf-covered border.

Sufficient evidence has now been given
showing that small objects left on the surface

of the land where worms abound soon get
buried, and that large stones sink slowly
downwards through the same means. Every
step of the process could be followed, from the
accidental deposition of a single casting on a
small object lying loose on the surface, to its
being entangled amidst the matted roots of
the turf, and lastly to its being embedded in
the mould at various depths beneath the
surface. When the same field was re-examined after the interval of a few years, such
objects were found at a greater depth than
before. The straightness and regularity of
the lines formed by the embedded objects,
and their parallelism with the surface of the
land, are the most striking features of the
case; for this parallelism shows how equably
the worms must have worked; the result
being, however, partly the effect of the washing down of the fresh castings by rain. The
specific gravity of the objects does not affect
their rate of sinking, as could be seen by
porous cinders, burnt marl, chalk and quartz
pebbles, having all sunk to the same depth
within the same time. Considering the
nature of the substratum, which at Leith Hill

Place was sandy soil including many bits of rock, and at Stonehenge, chalk-rubble with broken flints; considering, also, the presence of the turf-covered sloping border of mould round the great fragments of stone at both these places, their sinking does not appear to have been sensibly aided by their weight, though this was considerable.[*]

On the number of worms which live within a given space.—We will now show, firstly, what a vast number of worms live unseen by us beneath our feet, and, secondly, the actual weight of the earth which they bring up to the surface within a given space and within a given time.   Hensen, who has published so full and interesting an account of the habits of worms,[†] calculates, from the number which he found in a measured space, that there must exist 133,000 living worms in a hectare of

---

[*] Mr. R. Mallet remarks (' Quarterly Journal of Geolog. Soc., vol. xxxiii., 1877, p. 745) that " the extent to which the ground beneath the foundations of ponderous architectural structures, such as cathedral towers, has been known to become compressed, is as remarkable as it is instructive and curious.   The amount of depression in some cases may be measured by feet."   He instances the Tower of Pisa, but adds that it was founded on " dense clay."

[†] ' Zeitschrift für wissensch. Zoolog.' Bd. xxviii., 1877, p. 354

land, or 53,767 in an acre. This latter
number of worms would weigh 356 pounds,
taking Hensen's standard of the weight of a
single worm, namely, one gram. It should,
however, be noted that this calculation is
founded on the numbers found in a garden,
and Hensen believes that worms are here
twice as numerous as in corn-fields. The
above result, astonishing though it be, seems
to me credible, judging from the number of
worms which I have sometimes seen, and
from the number daily destroyed by birds
without the species being exterminated.
Some barrels of bad ale were left on Mr.
Miller's land,* in the hope of making vinegar,
but the vinegar proved bad, and the barrels
were upset. It should be premised that acetic
acid is so deadly a poison to worms that
Perrier found that a glass rod dipped into
this acid and then into a considerable body of
water in which worms were immersed, invariably killed them quickly. On the morning after the barrels had been upset, " the
" heaps of worms which lay dead on the

* See Mr. Dancer's paper in ' Proc. Phil. Soc. of Manchester,
1877, p. 248.

"ground were so amazing, that if Mr. Miller
"had not seen them, he could not have
"thought it possible for such numbers to
"have existed in the space."   As further evidence of the large number of worms which
live in the ground, Hensen states that he
found in a garden sixty-four open burrows in
a space of 14½ square feet, that is, nine in
2 square feet.   But the burrows are sometimes much more numerous, for when digging
in a grass-field near Maer Hall, I found a
cake of dry earth, as large as my two open
hands, which was penetrated by seven burrows, as large as goose-quills.

*Weight of the earth ejected from a single
burrow, and from all the burrows within a
given space.*—With respect to the weight of
the earth daily ejected by worms, Hensen
found that it amounted, in the case of some
worms which he kept in confinement, and
which he appears to have fed with leaves, to
only 0·5 gram, or less than 8 grains per
diem.   But a very much larger amount
must be ejected by worms in their natural
state, at the periods when they consume earth
as food instead of leaves, and when they are

making deep burrows. This is rendered almost certain by the following weights of the castings thrown up at the mouths of single burrows; the whole of which appeared to have been ejected within no long time, as was certainly the case in several instances. The castings were dried (excepting in one specified instance) by exposure during many days to the sun or before a hot fire.

WEIGHT OF THE CASTINGS ACCUMULATED AT THE MOUTH OF A SINGLE BURROW.

	Ounces.
(1.) Down, Kent (sub-soil red clay, full of flints, over-lying the chalk). The largest casting which I could find on the flanks of a steep valley, the sub-soil being here shallow. In this one case, the casting was not well dried	3·98
(2.) Down.—Largest casting which I could find (consisting chiefly of calcareous matter), on extremely poor pasture land at the bottom of the valley mentioned under (1.)	3·87
(3.) Down.—A large casting, but not of unusual size, from a nearly level field, poor pasture, laid down in grass about 35 years before..	1·22
(4.) Down.—Average weight of 11 not large castings ejected on a sloping surface on my lawn, after they had suffered some loss of weight from being exposed during a considerable length of time to rain ..	0·7
(5.) Near Nice in France.—Average weight of 12 castings of ordinary dimensions, collected by Dr. King on land which had not been mown for a long time and where worms abounded, viz., a lawn protected by shrubberies, near the sea; soil sandy and calcareous; these castings had been exposed for some time to rain, before being collected, and must have lost some weight by disintegration, but they still retained their form	1·37

WEIGHT OF THE CASTINGS ACCUMULATED AT THE MOUTH
OF A SINGLE BURROW—*continued.*

	Ounces.
(6.) The heaviest of the above twelve castings ..	1·76
(7.) Lower Bengal.—Average weight of 22 castings, collected by Mr. J. Scott, and stated by him to have been thrown up in the course of one or two nights	1·24
(8.) The heaviest of the above 22 castings	2·09
(9.) Nilgiri Mountains, S. India; average weight of the 5 largest castings collected by Dr. King. They had been exposed to the rain of the last monsoon, and must have lost some weight	3·15
(10.) The heaviest of the above 5 castings	4·34

In this table we see that castings which had been ejected at the mouth of the same burrow, and which in most cases appeared fresh and always retained their vermiform configuration, generally exceeded an ounce in weight after being dried, and sometimes nearly equalled a quarter of a pound. On the Nilgiri mountains one casting even exceeded this latter weight. The largest castings in England were found on extremely poor pasture-land; and these, as far as I have seen, are generally larger than those on land producing a rich vegetation. It would appear that worms have to swallow a greater amount of earth on poor than on rich land, in order to obtain sufficient nutriment.

With respect to the tower-like castings

near Nice (Nos. 5 and 6 in the above table),
Dr. King often found five or six of them on
a square foot of surface; and these, judging
from their average weight, would have
weighed together 7½ ounces; so that the
weight of those on a square yard would
have been 4 lb. 3½ oz. Dr. King collected,
near the close of the year 1872, all the
castings which still retained their vermiform
shape, whether broken down or not, from a
square foot, in a place abounding with worms,
on the summit of a bank, where no castings
could have rolled down from above. These
castings must have been ejected, as he judged
from their appearance in reference to the
rainy and dry periods near Nice, within the
previous five or six months; they weighed
9½ oz., or 5 lb. 5½ oz. per square yard. After
an interval of four months, Dr. King collected
all the castings subsequently ejected on the
same square foot of surface, and they weighed
2½ oz., or 1 lb. 6½ oz. per square yard.
Therefore within about ten months, or we
will say for safety's sake within a year, 12 oz.
of castings were thrown up on this one
square foot, or 6·75 pounds on the square

yard; and this would give 14·58 tons per acre.

In a field at the bottom of a valley in the chalk (see No. 2 in the foregoing table), a square yard was measured at a spot where very large castings abounded; they appeared, however, almost equally numerous in a few other places. These castings, which retained perfectly their vermiform shape, were collected; and they weighed when partially dried, 1 lb. 13½ oz. This field had been rolled with a heavy agricultural roller fifty-two days before, and this would certainly have flattened every single casting on the land. The weather had been very dry for two or three weeks before the day of collection, so that not one casting appeared fresh or had been recently ejected. We may therefore assume that those which were weighed had been ejected within, we will say, forty days from the time when the field was rolled,— that is, twelve days short of the whole intervening period. I had examined the same part of the field shortly before it was rolled, and it then abounded with fresh castings. Worms do not work in dry weather during the summer, or in winter during severe frosts. If we assume that they work for only half the year—though this is too low an estimate—then the worms in this field would eject during the year, 8·387 pounds per square yard; or 18·12 tons per acre, assuming the whole surface to be equally productive in castings.

In the foregoing cases some of the necessary data had to be estimated, but in the two following cases the results are much more trustworthy. A lady, on whose accuracy I can implicitly rely, offered to collect during a year all the castings thrown up on two separate square yards, near Leith Hill Place, in Surrey. The amount collected was, however, somewhat less than that originally ejected by the worms; for, as I have repeatedly observed, a good deal of the finest earth is washed away, whenever castings are thrown up during or shortly before heavy rain. Small portions also adhered to the surrounding blades of grass, and it required too much time to detach every one of them. On sandy soil, as in the present instance, castings are liable to crumble after dry weather, and particles were thus often lost. The lady also occasionally left home for a week or two, and at such times the castings must have suffered still greater loss from exposure to the weather. These losses were, however, compensated to some extent by the collections having been made on one of the squares for four days, and on the other square for two days more than the year.

A space was selected (October 9th, 1870) on a broad, grass-covered terrace, which had been mowed and swept during many years. It faced the south, but was shaded during part of the day by trees. It had been formed at least a century ago by a great accumulation of small and large fragments of sandstone, together with some sandy earth, rammed down level. It is probable that it was at first protected by being covered with turf. This terrace, judging from the number of castings on it, was rather unfavourable for the existence of worms, in comparison with the neighbouring fields and an upper terrace. It was indeed surprising that as many worms could live here as were seen; for on digging a hole in this terrace, the black vegetable mould together with the turf was only four inches in thickness, beneath which lay the level surface of light-coloured sandy soil, with many fragments of sandstone. Before any castings were collected all the previously existing ones were carefully removed. The last day's collection was on October 14th, 1871. The castings were then well dried before a fire; and they weighed exactly 3½ lbs. This would give for an acre of similar land 7·56 tons of dry earth annually ejected by worms.

The second square was marked on un-enclosed common land, at a height of about 700 ft. above the sea, at some little distance from Leith Hill Tower. The surface was clothed with short, fine turf, and had never been disturbed by the hand of man. The spot selected appeared neither particularly favourable nor the reverse for worms; but I have often noticed that castings are especially abundant on common land, and this may, perhaps, be attributed to the poorness of the soil. The vegetable mould was here between three and four inches in thickness. As this spot was at some distance from the

12

house where the lady lived, the castings were not collected at such short intervals of time as those on the terrace; consequently the loss of fine earth during rainy weather must have been greater in this than in the last case. The castings moreover were more sandy, and in collecting them during dry weather they sometimes crumbled into dust, and much was thus lost. Therefore it is certain that the worms brought up to the surface considerably more earth than that which was collected. The last collection was made on October 27th, 1871; i.e., 367 days after the square had been marked out and the surface cleared of all pre-existing castings. The collected castings, after being well dried, weighed 7·453 pounds; and this would give, for an acre of the same kind of land, 16·1 tons of annually ejected dry earth.

Summary of the four foregoing Cases.

(1.) Castings ejected near Nice within about a year, collected by Dr. King on a square foot of surface, calculated to yield per acre 14·58 tons.

(2.) Castings ejected during about 45 days on a square yard, in a field of poor pasture at the bottom of a large valley in the Chalk, calculated to yield annually per acre 18·12 tons.

(3.) Castings collected from a square yard on an old terrace at

Leith Hill Place, during 369 days, calculated to yield annually per acre 7·56 tons.

(4.) Castings collected from a square yard on Leith Hill Common during 367 days, calculated to yield annually per acre 16·1 tons.

The thickness of the layer of mould, which castings ejected during a year would form if uniformly spread out.—As we know from the two last cases in the above summary, the weight of the dried castings ejected by worms during a year on a square yard of surface, I wished to learn how thick a layer of ordinary mould this amount would form if spread uniformly over a square yard. The dry castings were therefore broken into small particles, and whilst being placed in a measure were well shaken and pressed down. Those collected on the Terrace amounted to 124·77 cubic inches; and this amount, if spread out over a square yard, would make a layer ·09612 inch in thickness. Those collected on the Common amounted to 197·56 cubic inches, and would make a similar layer ·1524 inch in thickness.

These thicknesses must, however, be corrected, for the triturated castings, after being well shaken down and pressed, did not make nearly so compact a mass as vegetable mould, though each separate particle was very compact. Yet mould is far from being compact, as is shown by the number of air-bubbles which rise up when the surface is flooded with water. It is moreover penetrated by many fine roots. To ascertain approximately by how much ordinary vegetable mould would be increased in bulk by being broken up into small particles and then dried, a thin oblong block of somewhat argillaceous mould (with the turf pared off) was measured before being broken up, was well dried and again measured. The drying caused it to shrink by $\frac{1}{7}$ of its original bulk, judging from exterior measurements alone. It was then triturated and partly reduced to powder, in the same manner as the castings had been treated, and its bulk now exceeded (notwithstanding shrinkage from drying) by $\frac{1}{16}$ that of the original block of damp mould. Therefore the above calculated thickness of the layer, formed by the castings from the Terrace, after being damped and spread over a square yard, would have to be reduced by $\frac{1}{16}$; and this will reduce the layer to ·09 of an inch, so that a layer ·9 inch in thickness would be formed in the course of ten years. On the same principle the castings from the Common would make in the course of a single year a layer ·1429 inch, or in the course of 10 years 1·429 inch, in thickness. We may say in round numbers that the thickness in the former case would amount to nearly 1 inch, and in the second case to nearly 1½ inch in 10 years.

In order to compare these results with those deduced from the rates at which small objects left on the surfaces of grass fields become buried (as described in the early part of this chapter), we will give the following summary :—

SUMMARY OF THE THICKNESS OF THE MOULD ACCUMULATED OVER OBJECTS LEFT STREWED ON THE SURFACE, IN THE COURSE OF TEN YEARS.

The accumulation of mould during 14⅓ years on the surface of a dry, sandy, grass-field near Maer Hall, amounted to 2·2 inches in 10 years.

The accumulation during 21¼ years on a swampy field near Maer Hall, amounted to nearly 1·9 inch in 10 years.

The accumulation during 7 years on a very swampy field near Maer Hall amounted to 2·1 inches in 10 years.

The accumulation during 29 years, on good, argillaceous pasture-land over the Chalk at Down, amounted to 2·2 inches in 10 years.

The accumulation during 30 years on the side of a valley over the Chalk at Down, the soil being argillaceous, very poor, and only just converted into pasture (so that it was for some years unfavourable for worms), amounted to 0·83 inches in 10 years.

In these cases (excepting the last) it may be seen that the amount of earth brought to the surface during 10 years is somewhat greater than that calculated from the castings which were actually weighed. This excess may be partly accounted for by the loss which the weighed castings had previously undergone through being washed by rain, by the adhesion of particles to the blades of the surrounding grass, and by their crumbling when dry. Nor must we overlook other agencies which in all ordinary cases add to the amount of mould, and which would not be included in the castings that were collected, namely, the fine earth brought up to the surface by burrowing larvæ and insects, especially by ants. The earth brought up by moles generally has a somewhat different appearance from vegetable mould; but after a time would not be distinguishable from it. In dry countries, moreover the wind plays an important part in carrying dust from one place to another, and even in England it must add to the mould on fields near great roads. But in our county these latter several agencies appear to be of quite subordinate importance in comparison with the action of worms.

We have no means of judging how great a weight of earth a single full-sized worm ejects during a year. Hensen estimates that 53,767 worms exist in an acre of land; but this is founded on the number found in gardens, and he believes that only about half as many live in corn-fields. How many live in old pasture land is unknown; but if we assume that half the above number, or 26,886 worms live on such land, then taking from the previous summary 15 tons as the weight of the castings annually thrown up on an acre of land, each worm must annually eject 20 ounces. A full-sized casting at the mouth of a single burrow often exceeds, as we have seen, an ounce in weight; and it is probable that worms eject more than 20 full-sized castings during a year. If they eject annually more than 20 ounces, we may infer that the worms which live in an acre of pasture land must be less than 26,886 in number.

Worms live chiefly in the superficial mould,

which is usually from 4 or 5 to 10 and even
12 inches in thickness; and it is this mould
which passes over and over again through
their bodies and is brought to the surface.
But worms occasionally burrow into the sub-
soil to a much greater depth, and on such
occasions they bring up earth from this
greater depth; and this process has gone on
for countless ages. Therefore the superficial
layer of mould would ultimately attain,
though at a slower and slower rate, a thickness equal to the depth to which worms
ever burrow, were there not other opposing
agencies at work which carry away to a
lower level some of the finest earth which is
continually being brought to the surface by
worms. How great a thickness vegetable
mould ever attains, I have not had good
opportunities for observing; but in the next
chapter, when we consider the burial of
ancient buildings, some facts will be given on
this head. In the two last chapters we
shall see that the soil is actually increased,
though only to a small degree, through the
agency of worms; but their chief work is
to sift the finer from the coarser particles, to

mingle the whole with vegetable débris, and to saturate it with their intestinal secretions.

Finally, no one who considers the facts given in this chapter—on the burying of small objects and on the sinking of great stones left on the surface—on the vast number of worms which live within a moderate extent of ground—on the weight of the castings ejected from the mouth of the same burrow—on the weight of all the castings ejected within a known time on a measured space—will hereafter, as I believe, doubt that worms play an important part in nature.

CHAPTER IV.

THE PART WHICH WORMS HAVE PLAYED IN THE BURIAL OF ANCIENT BUILDINGS.

The accumulation of rubbish on the sites of great cities independent of the action of worms—The burial of a Roman villa at Abinger—The floors and walls penetrated by worms—Subsidence of a modern pavement—The buried pavement at Beaulieu Abbey—Roman villas at Chedworth and Brading—The remains of the Roman town at Silchester—The nature of the débris by which the remains are covered—The penetration of the tesselated floors and walls by worms—Subsidence of the floors—Thickness of the mould—The old Roman city of Wroxeter—Thickness of the mould—Depth of the foundations of some of the Buildings—Conclusion.

ARCHÆOLOGISTS are probably not aware how much they owe to worms for the preservation of many ancient objects. Coins, gold ornaments, stone implements, &c., if dropped on the surface of the ground, will infallibly be buried by the castings of worms in a few years, and will thus be safely preserved, until the land at some future time is turned up For instance, many years ago a grass-field

was ploughed on the northern side of the
Severn, not far from Shrewsbury; and a
surprising number of iron arrow-heads were
found at the bottom of the furrows, which, as
Mr. Blakeway, a local antiquary, believed,
were relics of the battle of Shrewsbury in the
year 1403, and no doubt had been originally
left strewed on the battle-field.   In the
present chapter I shall show that not only
implements, &c., are thus preserved, but that
the floors and the remains of many ancient
buildings in England have been buried so
effectually, in large part through the action
of worms, that they have been discovered in
recent times solely through various accidents.
The enormous beds of rubbish, several yards
in thickness, which underlie many cities,
such as Rome, Paris, and London, the lower
ones being of great antiquity, are not here
referred to, as they have not been in any
way acted on by worms.   When we consider how much matter is daily brought into
a great city for building, fuel, clothing and
food, and that in old times when the roads
were bad and the work of the scavenger
was neglected, a comparatively small amount

was carried away, we may agree with
Elie de Beaumont, who, in discussing this
subject, says, " pour une voiture de matériaux
" qui en sort, on y en fait entrer cent." * Nor
should we overlook the effects of fires, the
demolition of old buildings, and the removal
of rubbish to the nearest vacant space.

Abinger, Surrey.—Late in the autumn of
1876, the ground in an old farm-yard at this
place was dug to a depth of 2 to $2\frac{1}{2}$ feet, and
the workmen found various ancient remains.
This led Mr. T. H. Farrer of Abinger Hall to
have an adjoining ploughed field searched.
On a trench being dug, a layer of concrete,
still partly covered with tesseræ (small red
tiles), and surrounded on two sides by broken-
down walls, was soon discovered. It is
believed † that this room formed part of the
atrium or reception-room of a Roman villa.
The walls of two or three other small rooms
were afterwards discovered. Many fragments
of pottery, other objects, and coins of several

---

* 'Leçons de Géologie pratique,' 1845, p. 142.

† A short account of this discovery was published in 'The
Times' of January 2, 1878; and a fuller account in 'The
Builder,' January 5, 1878.

Roman emperors, dating from 133 to 361, and perhaps to 375 A.D., were likewise found. Also a half-penny of George 1., 1715. The presence of this latter coin seems an anomaly; but no doubt it was dropped on the ground during the last century, and since then there has been ample time for its burial under a considerable depth of the castings of worms. From the different dates of the Roman coins we may infer that the building was long inhabited. It was probably ruined and deserted 1400 or 1500 years ago.

I was present during the commencement of the excavations (August 20, 1877) and Mr. Farrer had two deep trenches dug at opposite ends of the atrium, so that I might examine the nature of the soil near the remains. The field sloped from east to west at an angle of about 7°; and one of the two trenches, shown in the accompanying section (Fig. 8) was at the upper or eastern end. The diagram is on a scale of $\frac{1}{30}$ of an inch to an inch; but the trench, which was between 4 and 5 feet broad, and in parts above 5 feet deep, has necessarily been reduced out of all proportion. The fine mould over the floor

Fig. 8.

Section through the foundations of a buried Roman villa at
Abinger.   A A, vegetable mould; B, dark earth full of stones,
13 inches in thickness; C, black mould; D, broken mortar;
E, black mould; F F, undisturbed sub-soil; G, tesseræ; H.
concrete   I, nature unknown; W, buried wall.

of the atrium varied in thickness from 11
to 16 inches; and on the side of the trench in
the section was a little over 13 inches.   After
the mould had been removed, the floor
appeared as a whole moderately level; but it
sloped in parts at an angle of 1°, and in one
place near the outside at as much as 8° 30'·
The wall surrounding the pavement was
built of rough stones, and was 23 inches in
thickness where the trench was dug.   Its
broken summit was here 13 inches, but in
another part 15 inches, beneath the surface of
the field, being covered by this thickness of
mould.   In one spot, however, it rose to
within 6 inches of the surface.   On two
sides of the room, where the junction of the
concrete floor with the bounding walls could
be carefully examined, there was no crack or
separation.   This trench afterwards proved
to have been dug within an adjoining room
(11 ft. by 11 ft. 6 in. in size), the existence of
which was not even suspected whilst I was
present.

On the side of the trench farthest from the
buried wall (W), the mould varied from 9 to
14 inches in thickness; it rested on a mass (B)

23 inches thick of blackish earth, including many large stones.   Beneath this was a thin bed of very black mould (C), then a layer of earth full of fragments of mortar (D), and then another thin bed (about 3 inches thick) (F) of very black mould, which rested on the undisturbed subsoil (F) of firm, yellowish, argillaceous sand.   The 23-inch bed (B) was probably made ground, as this would have brought up the floor of the room to a level with that of the atrium.   The two thin beds of black mould at the bottom of the trench evidently marked two former land-surfaces. Outside the walls of the northern room, many bones, ashes, oyster-shells, broken pottery and an entire pot were subsequently found at a depth of 16 inches beneath the surface.

The second trench was dug on the western or lower side of the villa: the mould was here only 6½ inches in thickness, and it rested on a mass of fine earth full of stones, broken tiles and fragments of mortar, 34 inches in thickness, beneath which was the undisturbed sand.   Most of this earth had probably been washed down from the upper part of the field, and the fragments of stones, tiles, &c., must have come from the immediately adjoining ruins.

It appears at first sight a surprising fact that this field of light sandy soil should have been cultivated and ploughed during many years, and that not a vestige of these buildings should have been discovered. No one even suspected that the remains of a Roman villa lay hidden close beneath the surface. But the fact is less surprising when it is known that the field, as the bailiff believed, had never been ploughed to a greater depth than 4 inches. It is certain that when the land was first ploughed, the pavement and the surrounding broken walls must have been covered by at least 4 inches of soil, for otherwise the rotten concrete floor would have been scored by the ploughshare, the tesseræ torn up, and the tops of the old walls knocked down.

When the concrete and tesseræ were first cleared over a space of 14 by 9 ft., the floor which was coated with trodden-down earth exhibited no signs of having been penetrated by worms; and although the overlying fine mould closely resembled that which in many

13

places has certainly been accumulated by worms, yet it seemed hardly possible that this mould could have been brought up by worms from beneath the apparently sound floor. It seemed also extremely improbable that the thick walls, surrounding the room and still united to the concrete, had been undermined by worms, and had thus been caused to sink, being afterwards covered up by their castings. I therefore at first concluded that all the fine mould above the ruins had been washed down from the upper parts of the field; but we shall soon see that this conclusion was certainly erroneous, though much fine earth is known to be washed down from the upper part of the field in its present ploughed state during heavy rains.

Although the concrete floor did not at first appear to have been anywhere penetrated by worms, yet by the next morning little cakes of the trodden-down earth had been lifted up by worms over the mouths of seven burrows, which passed through the softer parts of the naked concrete, or between the interstices of the tesseræ. On the third morning twenty-five burrows were counted;

and by suddenly lifting up the little cakes of
earth, four worms were seen in the act
of quickly retreating. Two castings were
thrown up during the third night on the
floor, and these were of large size. The
season was not favourable for the full activity
of worms, and the weather had lately been
hot and dry, so that most of the worms now
lived at a considerable depth. In digging
the two trenches many open burrows and
some worms were encountered at between
30 and 40 inches beneath the surface ; but at
a greater depth they became rare. One
worm, however, was cut through at $48\frac{1}{2}$, and
another at $51\frac{1}{2}$ inches beneath the surface.
A fresh humus-lined burrow was also met
with at a depth of 57 and another at $65\frac{1}{2}$
inches. At greater depths than this, neither
burrows nor worms were seen.

As I wished to learn how many worms
lived beneath the floor of the atrium—a
space of about 14 by 9 feet—Mr. Farrer
was so kind as to make observations for
me, during the next seven weeks, by which
time the worms in the surrounding country
were in full activity, and were work-

ing near the surface. It is very improbable that worms should have migrated from the adjoining field into the small space of the atrium, after the superficial mould in which they prefer to live, had been removed. We may therefore conclude that the burrows and the castings which were seen here during the ensuing seven weeks were the work of the former inhabitants of the space. I will now give a few extracts from Mr. Farrer's notes.

Aug. 26th, 1877; that is, five days after the floor had been cleared. On the previous night there had been some heavy rain, which washed the surface clean, and now the mouths of forty burrows were counted. Parts of the concrete were seen to be solid, and had never been penetrated by worms, and here the rain-water lodged.

Sept. 5th.—Tracks of worms, made during the previous night, could be seen on the surface of the floor, and five or six vermiform castings had been thrown up. These were defaced.

Sept. 12th.—During the last six days, the worms have not been active, though many castings have been ejected in the neighbouring fields; but on this day the earth was a little raised over the mouths of the burrows, or castings were ejected, at ten fresh points. These were defaced.   It should be understood that when a fresh burrow is spoken of, this generally means only that an old burrow has been re-opened.   Mr. Farrer was repeatedly struck with the pertinacity with which the worms re-opened their old burrows, even when no earth was ejected from them.   I have often observed the same fact, and generally the mouths of the burrows are protected by an accumulation of pebbles, sticks or leaves. Mr. Farrer likewise observed that the worms living beneath the floor of the atrium often collected coarse grains of sand, and such little stones as they could find, round the mouths of their burrows.

Sept. 13th; soft wet weather.   The mouths of the burrows were re-opened, or castings were ejected, at 31 points; these were all defaced.

Sept. 14th; 34 fresh holes or castings all defaced.

Sept. 15th; 44 fresh holes, only 5 castings; all defaced.

Sept. 18th; 43 fresh holes, 8 castings; all defaced.

The number of castings on the surrounding fields was now very large.

Sept. 19th; 40 holes, 8 castings; all defaced.

Sept. 22nd; 43 holes, only a few fresh castings; all defaced.

Sept. 23rd; 44 holes, 8 castings.

Sept. 25th; 50 holes, no record of the number of castings.

Oct. 13th; 61 holes, no record of the number of castings.

After an interval of three years, Mr. Farrer, at my request, again looked at the concrete floor, and found the worms still at work.

Knowing what great muscular power worms possess, and seeing how soft the concrete was in many parts, I was not surprised at its having been penetrated by their burrows; but it is a more surprising fact that the mortar between the rough stones of the thick walls, surrounding the rooms, was found by Mr. Farrer to have been penetrated by worms. On August 26th, that is, five days after the ruins had been exposed, he observed four

open burrows on the broken summit of the
eastern wall (W in Fig. 8); and, on September 15th, other burrows similarly situated
were seen. It should also be noted that in
the perpendicular side of the trench (which
was much deeper than is represented in
Fig. 8) three recent burrows were seen, which
ran obliquely far down beneath the base of
the old wall.

We thus see that many worms lived beneath
the floor and the walls of the atrium at the
time when the excavations were made; and
that they afterwards almost daily brought up
earth to the surface from a considerable
depth. There is not the slightest reason to
doubt that worms have acted in this manner
ever since the period when the concrete was
sufficiently decayed to allow them to penetrate
it; and even before that period they would
have lived beneath the floor, as soon as it
became pervious to rain, so that the soil
beneath was kept damp. The floor and the
walls must therefore have been continually
undermined; and fine earth must have been
heaped on them during many centuries,
perhaps for a thousand years. If the burrows

beneath the floor and walls, which it is probable were formerly as numerous as they now are, had not collapsed in the course of time in the manner formerly explained, the underlying earth would have been riddled with passages like a sponge; and as this was not the case, we may feel sure that they have collapsed. The inevitable result of such collapsing during successive centuries, will have been the slow subsidence of the floor and of the walls, and their burial beneath the accumulated worm-castings. The subsidence of a floor, whilst it still remains nearly horizontal, may at first appear improbable; but the case presents no more real difficulty than that of loose objects strewed on the surface of a field, which, as we have seen, become buried several inches beneath the surface in the course of a few years, though still forming a horizontal layer parallel to the surface. The burial of the paved and level path on my lawn, which took place under my own observation, is an analogous case. Even those parts of the concrete floor which the worms could not penetrate would almost certainly have been undermined, and would have sunk, like the great stones at Leith Hill Place and Stonehenge, for the soil would have been damp beneath them. But the rate of sinking of the different parts would not have been quite equal, and the floor was not quite level. The foundations of the boundary walls lie, as shown in the section, at a very small depth beneath the surface; they would therefore have tended to subside at nearly the same rate as the floor. But this would not have occurred if the foundations had been deep, as in the case of some other Roman ruins presently to be described.

Finally, we may infer that a large part of the fine vegetable mould, which covered the floor and the broken-down walls of this villa, in some places to a thickness of 16 inches, was brought up from below by worms. From facts hereafter to be given there can be no doubt that some of the finest earth thus brought up will have been washed down the sloping surface of the field during every heavy shower of rain. If this had not occurred a greater amount of mould would have accumulated over the ruins than that now present. But beside the castings of worms and some

earth brought up by insects, and some accumulation of dust, much fine earth will have
been washed over the ruins from the upper
parts of the field, since it has been under
cultivation; and from over the ruins to the
lower parts of the slope; the present thickness of the mould being the resultant of these
several agencies.

I may here append a modern instance of
the sinking of a pavement, communicated to
me in 1871 by Mr. Ramsay, Director of the
Geological Survey of England. A passage
without a roof, 7 feet in length by 3 feet 2
inches in width, led from his house into the
garden, and was paved with slabs of Portland
stone. Several of these slabs were 16 inches
square, others larger, and some a little smaller.
This pavement had subsided about 3 inches
along the middle of the passage, and two
inches on each side, as could be seen by the
lines of cement by which the slabs had been
originally joined to the walls. The pavement had thus become slightly concave along
the middle; but there was no subsidence at
the end close to the house. Mr. Ramsay

could not account for this sinking, until he observed that castings of black mould were frequently ejected along the lines of junction between the slabs; and these castings were regularly swept away. The several lines of junction, including those with the lateral walls, were altogether 39 feet 2 inches in length. The pavement did not present the appearance of ever having been renewed, and the house was believed to have been built about eighty-seven years ago. Considering all these circumstances, Mr. Ramsay does not doubt that the earth brought up by the worms since the pavement was first laid down, or rather since the decay of the mortar allowed the worms to burrow through it, and therefore within a much shorter time than the eighty-seven years, has sufficed to cause the sinking of the pavement to the above amount, except close to the house, where the ground beneath would have been kept nearly dry.

Beaulieu Abbey, Hampshire.—This abbey was destroyed by Henry VIII., and there now remains only a portion of the southern aisle-wall. It is believed that the king had most of the stones carried away for building a castle; and it is certain that they have been removed.   The position of the nave-transept was ascertained not long ago by the foundations having been found; and the place is now marked by stones let into the ground.   Where the abbey formerly stood, there now extends a smooth grass-covered surface, which resembles in all respects the rest of the field.   The guardian, a very old man, said the surface had never been levelled in his time.   In the year 1853, the Duke of Buccleuch had three holes dug in the turf within a few yards of one another, at the western end of the nave; and the old tesselated pavement of the abbey was thus discovered.   These holes were afterwards surrounded by brickwork, and protected by trap-doors, so that the pavement might be readily inspected and preserved.   When my son William examined the place on January 5, 1872, he found that the pavement in the three holes lay at depths of $6\frac{3}{4}$, 10 and $11\frac{1}{2}$ inches beneath the surrounding turf-covered surface.   The old guardian asserted that he was often forced to remove worm-castings from the pavement; and that he had done

so about six months before.   My son collected
all from one of the holes, the area of which
was 5·32 square feet, and they weighed 7·97
ounces.   Assuming that this amount had
accumulated in six months, the accumulation
during a year on a square yard would be
1·68 pounds, which, though a large amount,
is very small compared with what, as we
have seen, is often ejected on fields and
commons.   When I visited the abbey on
June 22, 1877, the old man said that he had
cleared out the holes about a month before,
but a good many castings had since been
ejected.   I suspect that he imagined that he
swept the pavements oftener than he really
did, for the conditions were in several respects very unfavourable for the accumulation
of even a moderate amount of castings.   The
tiles are rather large, viz., about 5½ inches
square, and the mortar between them was in
most places sound, so that the worms were
able to bring up earth from below only at
certain points.   The tiles rested on a bed of
concrete, and the castings in consequence consisted in large part (viz., in the proportion
of 19 to 33) of particles of mortar, grains of

sand, little fragments of rock, bricks or tile ; and such substances could hardly be agreeable, and certainly not nutritious, to worms.

My son dug holes in several places within the former walls of the abbey, at a distance of several yards from the above described bricked squares.   He did not find any tiles, though these are known to occur in some other parts, but he came in one spot to concrete on which tiles had once rested. The fine mould beneath the turf on the sides of the several holes, varied in thickness from only 2 to $2\frac{3}{4}$ inches, and this rested on a layer from $8\frac{3}{4}$ to above 11 inches in thickness, consisting of fragments of mortar and stone-rubbish with the interstices compactly filled up with black mould. In the surrounding field, at a distance of 20 yards from the abbey, the fine vegetable mould was 11 inches thick.

We may conclude from these facts that when the abbey was destroyed and the stones removed, a layer of rubbish was left over the whole surface, and that as soon as the worms were able to penetrate the decayed concrete and the joints between the tiles, they slowly filled up the interstices in the overlying rubbish with their castings, which were after- wards accumulated to a thickness of nearly three inches over the whole surface. If we add to this latter amount the mould between the fragments of stones, some five or six inches of mould must have been brought up from beneath the concrete or tiles. The con- crete or tiles will consequently have subsided to nearly this amount. The bases of the columns of the aisles are now buried beneath mould and turf. It is not probable that they can have been undermined by worms, for their foundations would no doubt have been laid at a considerable depth. If they have not subsided, the stones of which the columns were constructed must have been removed from beneath the former level of the floor.

Chedworth, Gloucestershire.—The remains of a large Roman villa were discovered here in 1866, on ground which had been covered with wood from time immemorial. No suspicion seems ever to have been enter- tained that ancient buildings lay buried here, until a gamekeeper, in digging for rabbits, encountered some remains.* But subsequently the tops of some stone walls were detected in parts of the wood, projecting a little above the surface of the ground. Most of the coins found here belonged to Constans (who died 350 A.D.) and the Constantine family. My sons Francis and Horace visited the place in November 1877, for the sake of ascertaining what part worms may have played in the burial of these extensive remains. But the circumstances were not favourable for this object, as the ruins are surrounded on three sides by rather steep banks, down which earth is washed during rainy weather. Moreover most of the old rooms have been covered with roofs, for the protection of the elegant tesselated pavements.

A few facts may, however, be given on the thickness of the soil over these ruins. Close outside the northern rooms there is a broken wall, the summit of which was covered by 5

* Several accounts of these ruins have been published; the best is by Mr. James Farrer in 'Proc. Soc. of Antiquaries of Scotland,' vol. vi., Part II., 1867, p. 278. Also J. W. Grover, 'Journal of the British Arch. Assoc.' June 1866. Professor Buckman has likewise published a pamphlet, 'Notes on the Roman Villa at Chedworth,' 2nd edit. 1873: Cirencester.

inches of black mould; and in a hole dug on
the outer side of this wall, where the ground
had never before been disturbed, black mould,
full of stones, 26 inches in thickness, was
found, resting on the undisturbed sub-soil of
yellow clay. At a depth of 22 inches from
the surface a pig's jaw and a fragment of a
tile were found. When the excavations were
first made, some large trees grew over the
ruins; and the stump of one has been left
directly over a party-wall near the bath room,
for the sake of showing the thickness of the
superincumbent soil, which was here 38
inches. In one small room, which, after
being cleared out, had not been roofed over,
my sons observed the hole of a worm passing
through the rotten concrete, and a living
worm was found within the concrete. In
another open room worm-castings were seen
on the floor, over which some earth had by
this means been deposited, and here grass
now grew.

Brading, Isle of Wight.—A fine Roman
villa was discovered here in 1880; and by
the end of October no less than 18 chambers
had been more or less cleared. A coin dated

14

337 A.D. was found.   My son William visited
the place before the excavations were com-
pleted ; and he informs me that most of the
floors were at first covered with much rubbish
and fallen stones, having their interstices
completely filled up with mould, abounding
as the workmen said, with worms, above
which there was mould without any stones.
The whole mass was in most places from 3
to above 4 ft. in thickness.   In one very
large room the overlying earth was only
2 ft. 6 in. thick ; and after this had been removed, so many castings were thrown up
between the tiles that the surface had to
be almost daily swept.   Most of the floors
were fairly level.   The tops of the broken-
down walls were covered in some places by
only 4 or 5 inches of soil, so that they were
occasionally struck by the plough, but in
other places they were covered by from 13
to 18 inches of soil.   It is not probable that
these walls could have been undermined by
worms and subsided, as they rested on a
foundation of very hard red sand, into which
worms could hardly burrow.   The mortar,
however, between the stones of the walls of

a hypocaust was found by my son to have been penetrated by many worm-burrows. The remains of this villa stand on land which slopes at an angle of about 3°; and the land appears to have been long cultivated. Therefore no doubt a considerable quantity of fine earth has been washed down from the upper parts of the field, and has largely aided in the burial of these remains.

Silchester, Hampshire.—The ruins of this small Roman town have been better preserved than any other remains of the kind in England. A broken wall, in most parts from 15 to 18 feet in height and about 1½ mile in compass, now surrounds a space of about 100 acres of cultivated land, on which a farm-house and a church stand.* Formerly, when the weather was dry, the lines of the buried walls could be traced by the appearance of the crops; and recently very extensive excavations have been undertaken by the Duke of Wellington, under the superintendence of the late Rev. J. G. Joyce, by which means many large buildings have been

* These details are taken from the 'Penny Encyclopædia,' article, Hampshire.

discovered. Mr. Joyce made careful coloured sections, and measured the thickness of each bed of rubbish, whilst the excavations were in progress; and he has had the kindness to send me copies of several of them. When my sons Francis and Horace visited these ruins, he accompanied them, and added his notes to theirs.

Mr. Joyce estimates that the town was inhabited by the Romans for about three centuries; and no doubt much matter must have accumulated within the walls during this long period. It appears to have been destroyed by fire, and most of the stones used in the buildings have since been carried away. These circumstances are unfavourable for ascertaining the part which worms have played in the burial of the ruins; but as careful sections of the rubbish overlying an ancient town have seldom or never before been made in England, I will give copies of the most characteristic portions of some of those made by Mr. Joyce. They are of too great length to be here introduced entire.

An east and west section, 30 ft. in length, was made across a room in the Basilica, now

called the Hall of the Merchants (Fig. 9).
The hard concrete floor, still covered here
and there with tesseræ, was found at 3 ft.

Fig. 9.

Section within a room in the Basilica at Silchester.   Scale $\frac{1}{18}$.

beneath the surface of the field, which was here level. On the floor there were two large piles of charred wood, one alone of which is shown in the part of the section here given. This pile was covered by a thin white layer of decayed stucco or plaster, above which was a mass, presenting a singularly disturbed appearance, of broken tiles, mortar, rubbish and fine gravel, together 27 inches in thickness. Mr. Joyce believes that the gravel was used in making the mortar or concrete, which has since decayed, some of the lime probably having been dissolved. The disturbed state of the rubbish may have been due to its having been searched for building stones. This bed was capped by fine vegetable mould, 9 inches in thickness. From these facts we may conclude that the Hall was burnt down, and that much rubbish fell on the floor, through and from which the worms slowly brought up the mould, now forming the surface of the level field.

A section across the middle of another hall in the Basilica, 32 feet 6 inches in length, called the Œvarium, is shown in Fig. 10. It appears that we have here evidence of two fires, separated by an interval of time, during which the 6 inches of " mortar and concrete

Mould, 16 inches thick.

Charred wood, 10 inches thick.

Mortar with broken tiles, 6 inches thick.

Charred wood, 2 inches thick.

Rubble, 6 inches thick.

Undisturbed gravel.

Fig. 10.

Section within a hall in the Basilica at Silchester.   Scale $\frac{1}{11}$.

with broken tiles" was accumulated. Beneath one of the layers of charred wood, a valuable relic, a bronze eagle, was found; and this shows that the soldiers must have deserted the place in a panic. Owing to the death of Mr. Joyce, I have not been able to ascertain beneath which of the two layers the eagle was found. The bed of rubble overlying the undisturbed gravel originally formed, as I suppose, the floor, for it stands on a level with that of a corridor, outside the walls of the Hall; but the corridor is not shown in the section as here given. The vegetable mould was 16 inches thick in the thickest part; and the depth from the surface of the field, clothed with herbage, to the undisturbed gravel, was 40 inches.

The section shown in Fig. 11 represents an excavation made in the middle of the town, and is here introduced because the bed of " rich" "mould" attained, according to Mr. Joyce, the unusual thickness of 20 inches. Gravel lay at the depth of 48 inches from the surface but it was not ascertained whether this was in its natural state, or had been brought here and had been rammed down, as occurs in some other places.

The section shown in Fig. 12 was taken in the centre of the Basilica, and though it was 5 feet in depth, the natural sub-soil was not

Mould, 20 inches thick.

Rubble with broken tiles, 4 inches thick.

Black decayed wood, in thickest part 6 inches thick.

Gravel.

Fig. 11.

Section in a block of buildings in the middle of the town of Silchester.

reached. The bed marked " concrete " was probably at one time a floor ; and the beds beneath seem to be the remnants of more ancient buildings. The vegetable mould was

here only 9 inches thick. In some other
sections, not copied, we likewise have

Mould, 9 inches thick.

Light-coloured earth with
large pieces of broken
tiles, 7 inches.

Dark, fine-grained rubbish
with small bits of tiles
20 inches.

Concrete, 4 inches.

Stucco, 2 inches.

Made bottom with frag-
ments of tiles, 8 inches.

Fine-grained made ground,
with the débris of older
buildings.

Fig. 12.

Section in the centre of the Basilica at Silchester.

evidence of buildings having been erected
over the ruins of older ones. In one case

there was a layer of yellow clay of very unequal thickness between two beds of débris, the lower one of which rested on a floor with tesseræ.   The old broken walls appear sometimes to have been roughly cut down to a uniform level, so as to serve as the foundations of a temporary building; and Mr. Joyce suspects that some of these buildings were wattled sheds, plastered with clay, which would account for the above-mentioned layer of clay.

Turning now to the points which more immediately concern us.   Worm-castings were observed on the floors of several of the rooms, in one of which the tesselation was unusually perfect.   The tesseræ here consisted of little cubes of hard sandstone of about 1 inch, several of which were loose or projected slightly above the general level One or occasionally two open worm-burrows were found beneath all the loose tesseræ. Worms have also penetrated the old walls of these ruins.   A wall, which had just been exposed to view during the excavations then in progress, was examined: it was built of large flints, and was 18 inches in thickness.

It appeared sound, but when the soil was removed from beneath, the mortar in the lower part was found to be so much decayed that the flints fell apart from their own weight. Here, in the middle of the wall, at a depth of 29 inches beneath the old floor and of $49\frac{1}{2}$ inches beneath the surface of the field, a living worm was found, and the mortar was penetrated by several burrows.

A second wall was exposed to view for the first time, and an open burrow was seen on its broken summit. By separating the flints this burrow was traced far down in the interior of the wall; but as some of the flints cohered firmly, the whole mass was disturbed in pulling down the wall, and the burrow could not be traced to the bottom. The foundations of a third wall, which appeared quite sound, lay at a depth of 4 feet beneath one of the floors, and of course at a considerably greater depth beneath the level of the ground. A large flint was wrenched out of the wall at about a foot from the base, and this required much force, as the mortar was sound; but behind the flint in the middle of the wall, the mortar was friable,

and here there were worm-burrows. Mr.
Joyce and my sons were surprised at the
blackness of the mortar in this and in several
other cases, and at the presence of mould in
the interior of the walls. Some may have
been placed there by the old builders instead
of mortar; but we should remember that
worms line their burrows with black humus.
Moreover open spaces would almost certainly
have been occasionally left between the large
irregular flints; and these spaces, we may
feel sure, would be filled up by the worms
with their castings, as soon as they were able
to penetrate the wall. Rain-water, oozing
down the burrows would also carry fine
dark-coloured particles into every crevice.
Mr. Joyce was at first very sceptical about
the amount of work which I attributed to
worms; but he ends his notes with reference
to the last-mentioned wall by saying, " This
" case caused me more surprise and brought
" more conviction to me than any other. I
" should have said, and did say, that it was
" quite impossible such a wall could have been
" penetrated by earth-worms."

In almost all the rooms the pavement has

South.

Horizontal line.

North.

Fig. 13.

Section of the subsided floor of a room, paved with tesseræ, at Silchester.   Scale $\frac{1}{70}$.

sunk considerably, especially towards the middle; and this is shown in the three following sections. The measurements were made by stretching a string tightly and horizontally over the floor. The section, Fig. 13, was taken from north to south across a room, 18 feet 4 inches in length, with a nearly perfect pavement, next to the "Red Wooden Hut." In the northern half, the subsidence amounted to $5\frac{3}{4}$ inches beneath the level of the floor as it now stands close to the walls; and it was greater in the northern than in the southern half; but, according to Mr. Joyce, the entire pavement has obviously subsided. In several places, the tesseræ appeared as if drawn a little away from the walls; whilst in other places they were still in close contact with them.

In Fig. 14, we see a section across the paved floor of the southern corridor or ambulatory of a quadrangle, in an excavation made near "The Spring." The floor is 7 feet 9 inches wide, and the broken-down walls now project only $\frac{3}{4}$ of an inch above its level. The field, which was in pasture, here sloped from north to south, at an angle of 3° 40'. The nature of the ground on each side of the corridor is shown in the section. It consisted of earth full of stones and other débris, capped with dark vegetable mould which was thicker on the lower or southern than on the northern side. The pavement was nearly level along lines parallel to the side-walls, but had sunk in the middle as much as $7\frac{3}{4}$ inches.

A small room at no great distance from that represented in Fig. 13, had been enlarged by the Roman occupier on the southern side, by an addition of 5 feet 4 inches in breadth. For this purpose the southern wall of the house had been pulled down, but the foundations f the old wall had been left buried at a little depth

Fig. 14.

A north and south section through the subsided floor of a corridor, paved with tesserae. Outside the broken-down bounding walls, the excavated ground on each side is shown for a short space. Nature of the ground beneath the tesserae unknown. Silchester. Scale $\frac{1}{20}$.

beneath the pavement of the enlarged room. Mr. Joyce believes that this buried wall must have been built before the reign of Claudius II., who died 270, A.D. We see in the accompanying section, Fig. 15, that the tesselated pavement has subsided to a less degree over the buried wall than elsewhere; so that a slight convexity or protuberance here stretched in a straight line across the room. This led to a hole being dug, and the buried wall was thus discovered.

We see in these three sections, and in several others not given, that the old pavements have sunk or sagged considerably. Mr. Joyce formerly attributed this sinking solely to the slow settling of the ground. That there has been some settling is highly probable, and it may be seen in section 15 that the pavement for a width of 5 feet over the southern enlargement of the room, which must have been built on fresh ground, has sunk a little more than on the old northern side. But this sinking may possibly have had no connection with the enlargement of the room, for in Fig. 13, one half of the pavement has subsided more

15

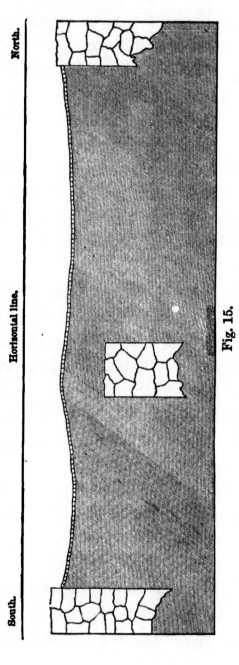

Fig. 15.

Section through the subsided floor, paved with tesseræ, and of the broken-down bounding walls of a room at Silchester, which had been formerly enlarged, with the foundations of the old wall left buried. Scale $\frac{1}{40}$.

than the other half without any assignable
cause. In a bricked passage to Mr. Joyce's
own house, laid down only about six years
ago, the same kind of sinking has occurred as
in the ancient buildings. Nevertheless it does
not appear probable that the whole amount
of sinking can be thus accounted for. The
Roman builders excavated the ground to an
unusual depth for the foundations of their
walls, which were thick and solid; it is
therefore hardly credible that they should
have been careless about the solidity of the
bed on which their tesselated and often
ornamented pavements were laid. The sinking must, as it appears to me, be attributed
in chief part to the pavement having been
undermined by worms, which we know are
still at work. Even Mr. Joyce at last admitted that this could not have failed to have
produced a considerable effect. Thus also the
large quantity of fine mould overlying the
pavements can be accounted for, the presence
of which would otherwise be inexplicable. My
sons noticed that in one room in which the
pavement had sagged very little, there was an
unusually small amount of overlying mould.

As the foundations of the walls generally
lie at a considerable depth, they will either
have not subsided at all through the under-
mining action of worms, or they will have
subsided much less than the floor. This
latter result would follow from worms not
often working deep down beneath the foundations; but more especially from the walls not
yielding when penetrated by worms, whereas
the successively formed burrows in a mass
of earth, equal to one of the walls in depth
and thickness, would have collapsed many
times since the desertion of the ruins,
and would consequently have shrunk or
subsided. As the walls cannot have sunk
much or at all, the immediately adjoining
pavement from adhering to them will have
been prevented from subsiding; and thus
the present curvature of the pavement is
intelligible.

The circumstance which has surprised me
most with respect to Silchester is that during
the many centuries which have elapsed since
the old buildings were deserted, the vegetable
mould has not accumulated over them to a
greater thickness than that here observed. In

most places it is only about 9 inches in thickness, but in some places 12 or even more inches. In Fig. 11, it is given as 20 inches, but this section was drawn by Mr. Joyce before his attention was particularly called to this subject. The land enclosed within the old walls is described as sloping slightly to the south; but there are parts which, according to Mr. Joyce, are nearly level, and it appears that the mould is here generally thicker than elsewhere. The surface slopes in other parts from west to east, and Mr. Joyce describes one floor as covered at the western end by rubbish and mould to a thickness of $28\frac{1}{2}$ inches, and at the eastern end by a thickness of only $11\frac{1}{2}$ inches. A very slight slope suffices to cause recent castings to flow downwards during heavy rain, and thus much earth will ultimately reach the neighbouring rills and streams and be carried away. By this means, the absence of very thick beds of mould over these ancient ruins may, as I believe, be explained. Moreover most of the land here has long been ploughed, and this would greatly aid the washing away of the finer earth during rainy weather.

The nature of the beds immediately
beneath the vegetable mould in some of the
sections is rather perplexing. We see, for
instance, in the section of an excavation in a
grass meadow (Fig. 14), which sloped from
north to south at an angle of 3° 40', that the
mould on the upper side is only six inches
and on the lower side nine inches in thickness. But this mould lies on a mass (25¼
inches in thickness on the upper side) " of
" dark brown mould," as described by Mr.
Joyce, " thickly interspersed with small
" pebbles and bits of tiles, which present a
" corroded or worn appearance." The state
of this dark-coloured earth is like that of a
field which has long been ploughed, for the
earth thus becomes intermingled with stones
and fragments of all kinds which have been
much exposed to the weather. If during the
course of many centuries this grass meadow
and the other now cultivated fields have been
at times ploughed, and at other times left as
pasture, the nature of the ground in the above
section is rendered intelligible. For worms
will continually have brought up fine earth
from below, which will have been stirred

up by the plough whenever the land was cultivated. But after a time a greater thickness of fine earth will thus have been accumulated than could be reached by the plough; and a bed like the 25½-inch mass, in Fig. 14, will have been formed beneath the superficial mould, which latter will have been brought to the surface within more recent times, and have been well sifted by the worms.

Wroxeter, Shropshire.—The old Roman city of Uriconium was founded in the early part of the second century, if not before this date; and it was destroyed, according to Mr. Wright, probably between the middle of the fourth and fifth century. The inhabitants were massacred, and skeletons of women were found in the hypocausts. Before the year 1859, the sole remnant of the city above ground, was a portion of a massive wall about 20 ft. in height. The surrounding land undulates slightly, and has long been under cultivation. It had been noticed that the corn-crops ripened prematurely in certain narrow lines, and that the snow remained unmelted in certain places longer than in others.

These appearances led, as I was informed, to extensive excavations being undertaken. The foundations of many large buildings and several streets have thus been exposed to view. The space enclosed within the old walls is an irregular oval, about 1¾ mile in length. Many of the stones or bricks used in the buildings must have been carried away; but the hypocausts, baths, and other underground buildings were found tolerably perfect, being filled with stones, broken tiles, rubbish and soil. The old floors of various rooms were covered with rubble. As I was anxious to know how thick the mantle of mould and rubbish was, which had so long concealed these ruins, I applied to Dr. H. Johnson, who had superintended the excavations; and he, with the greatest kindness, twice visited the place to examine it in reference to my questions, and had many trenches dug in four fields which had hitherto been undisturbed. The results of his observations are given in the following Table. He also sent me specimens of the mould, and answered, as far as he could, all my questions.

MEASUREMENTS BY DR. H. JOHNSON OF THE THICKNESS OF THE VEGETABLE MOULD OVER THE ROMAN RUINS AT WROXETER.

Trenches dug in a field called "Old Works."

		Thickness of mould in inches.
1. At a depth of 36 inches undisturbed sand was reached		20
2. At a depth of 33 inches concrete was reached		21
3. „ „ 9 inches concrete was reached		9

Trenches dug in a field called "Shop "Leasows;" this is the highest field within the old walls, and slopes down from a sub-central point on all sides at about an angle of 2°.

	Thickness of mould in inches.
4. Summit of field, trench 45 inches deep ..	40
5. Close to summit of field, trench 36 inches deep	26
6. „ „ trench 28 inches deep	28
7. Near summit of field, trench 36 inches deep	24
8. „ „ trench at one end 39 inches deep; the mould here graduated into the underlying undisturbed sand, and its thickness is somewhat arbitrary. At the other end of the trench, a causeway was encountered at a depth of only 7 inches, and the mould was here only 7 inches thick ..	24
9. Trench close to the last, 28 inches in depth ..	15
10 Lower part of same field, trench 30 inches deep	15
11 „ „ trench 31 inches deep	17
12. „ „ trench 36 inches deep, at which depth undisturbed sand was reached	28

Thickness
of mould in
inches.

13. In another part of same field, trench 9½ inches
    deep, stopped by concrete 9½

14. In another part of same field, trench 9 inches
    deep, stopped by concrete 9

15. In another part of the same field, trench 24
    inches deep, when sand was reached .. 16

16. In another part of same field, trench 30 inches
    deep, when stones were reached; at one end
    of the trench mould 12 inches, at the other
    end 14 inches thick 13

Small field between "Old Works" and
"Shop Leasows," I believe nearly as high as
the upper part of the latter field.

Thickness
of mould in
inches.

17. Trench 26 inches deep 24

18.   „   10 inches deep, and then came upon a
      causeway 10

19. Trench 34 inches deep 30

20.   „   31 inches deep.. 31

Field on the western side of the space
enclosed within the old walls.

Thickness
of mould in
inches

21. Trench 28 inches deep, when undisturbed sand
    was reached 16

22. Trench 29 inches deep, when undisturbed sand
    was reached 15

23. Trench 14 inches deep, and then came upon a
    building 14

Dr. Johnson distinguished as mould the
earth which differed, more or less abruptly, in

its dark colour and in its texture from the underlying sand or rubble.   In the specimens sent to me, the mould resembled that which lies immediately beneath the turf in old pasture-land, excepting that it often contained small stones, too large to have passed through the bodies of worms.   But the trenches above described were dug in fields, none of which were in pasture, and all had been long cultivated.   Bearing in mind the remarks made in reference to Silchester on the effects of long-continued culture, combined with the action of worms in bringing up the finer particles to the surface, the mould, as so designated by Dr. Johnson, seems fairly well to deserve its name.   Its thickness, where there was no causeway, floor or walls beneath, was greater than has been elsewhere observed, namely in many places above 2 ft., and in one spot above 3 ft.   The mould was thickest on and close to the nearly level summit of the field called "Shop Leasows," and in a small adjoining field, which, as I believe, is of nearly the same height.   One side of the former field slopes at an angle of rather above 2°, and I should have expected that

the mould, from being washed down during
heavy rain, would have been thicker in the
lower than in the upper part; but this was
not the case in two out of the three trenches
here dug.

In many places, where streets ran beneath
the surface, or where old buildings stood, the
mould was only 8 inches in thickness; and
Dr. Johnson was surprised that in ploughing
the land, the ruins had never been struck by
the plough as far as he had heard. He thinks
that when the land was first cultivated the old
walls were perhaps intentionally pulled down,
and that hollow places were filled up. This
may have been the case; but if after the
desertion of the city the land was left for
many centuries uncultivated, worms would
have brought up enough fine earth to have
covered the ruins completely ; that is if
they had subsided from having been undermined. The foundations of some of the walls,
for instance those of the portion still standing about 20 feet above the ground, and
those of the market-place, lie at the extraordinary depth of 14 feet; but it is highly
improbable that the foundations were gener-

ally so deep. The mortar employed in the buildings must have been excellent, for it is still in parts extremely hard. Wherever walls of any height have been exposed to view, they are, as Dr. Johnson believes, still perpendicular. The walls with such deep foundations cannot have been undermined by worms, and therefore cannot have subsided, as appears to have occurred at Abinger and Silchester. Hence it is very difficult to account for their being now completely covered with earth; but how much of this covering consists of vegetable mould and how much of rubble I do not know. The market-place, with the foundations at a depth of 14 feet, was covered up, as Dr. Johnson believes, by between 6 and 24 inches of earth. The tops of the broken-down walls of a caldarium or bath, 9 feet in depth, were likewise covered up with nearly 2 feet of earth. The summit of an arch, leading into an ash-pit 7 feet in depth, was covered up with not more than 8 inches of earth. Whenever a building which has not subsided is covered with earth, we must suppose, either that the upper layers of stone have been at

some time carried away by man, or that earth
has since been washed down during heavy
rain, or blown down during storms, from the
adjoining land; and this would be especially
apt to occur where the land has long been
cultivated.   In the above cases the adjoining
land is somewhat higher than the three specified sites, as far as I can judge by maps and
from information given me by Dr. Johnson.
If, however, a great pile of broken stones
mortar, plaster, timber and ashes fell over the
remains of any building, their disintegration
in the course of time, and the sifting action
of worms, would ultimately conceal the whole
beneath fine earth.

Conclusion.—The cases given in this chapter
show that worms have played a considerable
part in the burial and concealment of several
Roman and other old buildings in England;
but no doubt the washing down of soil from
the neighbouring higher lands, and the deposition of dust, have together aided largely
in the work of concealment.   Dust would be
apt to accumulate wherever old broken-down
walls projected a little above the then exist-

ing surface and thus afforded some shelter. The floors of the old rooms, halls and passages have generally sunk, partly from the settling of the ground, but chiefly from having been undermined by worms; and the sinking has commonly been greater in the middle than near the walls.   The walls themselves, whenever their foundations do not lie at a great depth, have been penetrated and undermined by worms, and have consequently subsided. The unequal subsidence thus caused, probably explains the great cracks which may be seen in many ancient walls, as well as their inclination from the perpendicular.

CHAPTER V.

THE ACTION OF WORMS IN THE DENUDATION OF THE LAND.

Evidence of the amount of denudation which the land has undergone—Subaerial denudation—The deposition of dust—Vegetable mould, its dark colour and fine texture largely due to the action of worms—The disintegration of rocks by the humus-acids—Similar acids apparently generated within the bodies of worms—The action of these acids facilitated by the continued movement of the particles of earth—A thick bed of mould checks the disintegration of the underlying soil and rocks. Particles of stone worn or triturated in the gizzards of worms—Swallowed stones serve as mill-stones—The levigated state of the castings—Fragments of brick in the castings over ancient buildings well rounded. The triturating power of worms not quite insignificant under a geological point of view.

No one doubts that our world at one time consisted of crystalline rocks, and that it is to their disintegration through the action of air, water, changes of temperature, rivers, waves of the sea, earthquakes and volcanic outbursts, that we owe our sedimentary formations. These after being consolidated and sometimes

recrystallized, have often been again disintegrated. Denudation means the removal
of such disintegrated matter to a lower level.
Of the many striking results due to the
modern progress of geology there are hardly
any more striking than those which relate to
denudation. It was long ago seen that
there must have been an immense amount
of denudation; but until the successive formations were carefully mapped and measured,
no one fully realised how great was the
amount. One of the first and most remarkable memoirs ever published on this subject
was that by Ramsay,* who in 1846 showed
that in Wales from 9000 to 11,000 feet in
thickness of solid rock had been stripped off
large tracks of country. Perhaps the plainest
evidence of great denudation is afforded by
faults or cracks, which extend for many miles
across certain districts, with the strata on one
side raised even ten thousand feet above the
corresponding strata on the opposite side; and
yet there is not a vestige of this gigantic
displacement visible on the surface of the

* "On the denudation of South Wales," &c., 'Memoirs of the
Geological Survey of Great Britain,' vol. i., p. 297, 1846.

land. A huge pile of rock has been planed
away on one side and not a remnant left.

Until the last twenty or thirty years, most
geologists thought that the waves of the sea
were the chief agents in the work of denudation ; but we may now feel sure that air and
rain, aided by streams and rivers, are much
more powerful agents,—that is if we consider
the whole area of the land.   The long lines of
escarpment which stretch across several parts
of England were formerly considered to be
undoubtedly ancient coast-lines; but we now
know that they stand up above the general
surface merely from resisting air, rain and
frost better than the adjoining formations.
It has rarely been the good fortune of a
geologist to bring conviction to the minds of
his fellow-workers on a disputed point by a
single memoir; but Mr. Whitaker, of the
Geological Survey of England, was so for-
tunate when, in 1867, he published his paper
" On sub-aerial Denudation, and on Cliffs and
Escarpments of the Chalk." *   Before this

* 'Geological Magazine,' October and November, 1867, vol.
iv. pp. 447 and 483. Copious references on the subject are given
in this remarkable memoir.

paper appeared, Mr. A. Tylor had adduced important evidence on sub-aerial denudation, by showing that the amount of matter brought down by rivers must infallibly lower the level of their drainage-basins by many feet in no immense lapse of time. This line of argument has since been followed up in the most interesting manner by Archibald Geikie, Croll and others, in a series of valuable memoirs.* For the sake of those who have never attended to this subject, a single instance may be here given, namely that of the Mississippi, which is chosen because the amount of sediment brought down by this great river has been investigated with especial care by order of the United States Government. The result is, as Mr. Croll shows, that the mean level of its enormous area of

---

* A. Tylor "On changes of the sea-level," &c., 'Philosophical Mag.' (Ser. 4th) vol. v., 1853, p. 258. Archibald Geikie, Transactions Geolog. Soc. of Glasgow, vol. iii., p. 153 (read March, 1868). Croll "On Geological Time," 'Philosophical Mag.', May, August, and November, 1868. See also Croll, 'Climate and Time,' 1875, Chap. XX. For some recent information on the amount of sediment brought down by rivers, see 'Nature,' Sept. 23rd, 1880. Mr. T. Mellard Reade has published some interesting articles on the astonishing amount of matter brought down in solution by rivers. See Address, Geolog. Soc., Liverpool, 1876–77.

drainage must be lowered $\frac{1}{4566}$ of a foot annually, or 1 foot in 4566 years. Consequently, taking the best estimate of the mean height of the North American continent, viz. 748 feet, and looking to the future, the whole of the great Mississippi basin will be washed away, and " brought down to the sea-"level in less than 4,500,000 years, if no " elevation of the land takes place." Some rivers carry down much more sediment relatively to their size, and some much less than the Mississippi.

Disintegrated matter is carried away by the wind as well as by running water During volcanic outbursts much rock is triturated and is thus widely dispersed; and in all arid countries the wind plays an important part in the removal of such matter. Wind-driven sand also wears down the hardest rocks. I have shown [*] that during four months of the year a large quantity of dust is blown from the north-western shores of Africa, and falls on the Atlantic over a

* " An account of the fine dust which often falls on Vessels in the Atlantic Ocean," Proc. Geolog. Soc. of London, June 4th, 1845.

space of 1600 miles in latitude, and for a distance of from 300 to 600 miles from the coast. But dust has been seen to fall at a distance of 1030 miles from the shores of Africa. During a stay of three weeks at St. Jago in the Cape Verde Archipelago, the atmosphere was almost always hazy, and extremely fine dust coming from Africa was continually falling. In some of this dust which fell in the open ocean at a distance of between 330 and 380 miles from the African coast, there were many particles of stone, about $\frac{1}{1000}$ of an inch square. Nearer to the coast the water has been seen to be so much discoloured by the falling dust, that a sailing vessel left a track behind her. In countries, like the Cape Verde Archipelago, where it seldom rains and there are no frosts, the solid rock nevertheless disintegrates ; and in conformity with the views lately advanced by a distinguished Belgian geologist, De Koninck, such disintegration may be attributed in chief part to the action of the carbonic and nitric acids, together with the nitrates and nitrites of ammonia, dissolved in the dew.

In all humid, even moderately humid,

countries, worms aid in the work of denudation in several ways. The vegetable mould which covers, as with a mantle, the surface of the land, has all passed many times through their bodies. Mould differs in appearance from the subsoil only in its dark colour, and in the absence of fragments or particles of stone (when such are present in the subsoil), larger than those which can pass through the alimentary canal of a worm. This sifting of the soil is aided, as has already been remarked, by burrowing animals of many kinds, especially by ants. In countries where the summer is long and dry, the mould in protected places must be largely increased by dust blown from other and more exposed places. For instance, the quantity of dust sometimes blown over the plains of La Plata, where there are no solid rocks, is so great, that during the " gran seco," 1827 to 1830, the appearance of the land, which is here unenclosed, was so completely changed that the inhabitants could not recognise the limits of their own estates, and endless lawsuits arose. Immense quantities of dust are likewise blown about in Egypt and in the

south of France. In China, as Richthofen
maintains, beds appearing like fine sediment,
several hundred feet in thickness and extend-
ing over an enormous area, owe their origin
to dust blown from the high lands of central
Asia.* In humid countries like Great
Britain, as long as the land remains in its
natural state clothed with vegetation, the
mould in any one place can hardly be much
increased by dust; but in its present condition, the fields near high roads, where there
is much traffic, must receive a considerable
amount of dust, and when fields are harrowed
during dry and windy weather, clouds of dust
may be seen to be blown away. But in all
these cases the surface-soil is merely transported from one place to another. The dust
which falls so thickly within our houses con-

* For La Plata, see my 'Journal of Researches,' during the
voyage of the *Beagle*, 1845, p. 133. Élie de Beaumont has
given ('Leçons de Géolog. pratique,' tom. I. 1845, p. 183) an
excellent account of the enormous quantity of dust which is
transported in some countries. I cannot but think that Mr.
Proctor has somewhat exaggerated ('Pleasant Ways in Science,'
1879, p. 379) the agency of dust in a humid country like Great
Britain. James Geikie has given ('Prehistoric Europe,' 1880,
p. 165) a full abstract of Richthofen's views, which, however,
he disputes.

sists largely of organic matter, and if spread over the land would in time decay and disappear almost entirely. It appears, however, from recent observations on the snow-fields of the Arctic regions, that some little meteoric dust of extra mundane origin is continually falling.

The dark colour of ordinary mould is obviously due to the presence of decaying organic matter, which, however, is present in but small quantities. The loss of weight which mould suffers when heated to redness seems to be in large part due to water in combination being dispelled. In one sample of fertile mould the amount of organic matter was ascertained to be only 1·76 per cent.; in some artificially prepared soil it was as much as 5·5 per cent., and in the famous black soil of Russia from 5 to even 12 per cent.* In leaf-mould formed exclusively by the decay of leaves the amount is much greater, and in peat the carbon alone sometimes amounts to

---

* These statements are taken from Von Hensen in 'Zeitschrift für wissenschaft. Zoologie,' Bd. xxviii., 1877, p. 360. Those with respect to peat are taken from Mr. A. A. Julien in 'Proc. American Assoc. Science, 1879, p. 314.

64 per cent.; but with these latter cases we
are not here concerned. The carbon in the
soil tends gradually to oxidise and to disappear, except where water accumulates and
the climate is cool;* so that in the oldest
pasture-land there is no great excess of
organic matter, notwithstanding the continued decay of the roots and the underground
stems of plants, and the occasional addition
of manure. The disappearance of the organic
matter from mould is probably much aided
by its being brought again and again to the
surface in the castings of worms.

Worms, on the other hand, add largely to
the organic matter in the soil by the astonishing number of half-decayed leaves which
they draw into their burrows to a depth of 2
or 3 inches. They do this chiefly for obtaining food, but partly for closing the mouths
of their burrows and for lining the upper
part. The leaves which they consume are
moistened, torn into small shreds, partially
digested, and intimately commingled with

* I have given some facts on the climate necessary or favourable for the formation of peat, in my ' Journal of Researches,
1845, p. 287.

earth ; and it is this process which gives to vegetable mould its uniform dark tint. It is known that various kinds of acids are generated by the decay of vegetable matter; and from the contents of the intestines of worms and from their castings being acid, it seems probable that the process of digestion induces an analogous chemical change in the swallowed, triturated, and half decayed leaves. The large quantity of carbonate of lime secreted by the calciferous glands apparently serves to neutralise the acids thus generated; for the digestive fluid of worms will not act unless it be alkaline. As the contents of the upper part of their intestines are acid, the acidity can hardly be due to the presence of uric acid. We may therefore conclude that the acids in the alimentary canal of worms are formed during the digestive process; and that probably they are nearly of the same nature as those in ordinary humus. The latter are well known to have the power of de-oxidising or dissolving peroxide of iron, as may be seen wherever peat overlies red sand, or where a rotten root penetrates such sand. Now I kept some worms in a pot filled with very fine reddish sand, consisting of minute particles of silex coated with the red oxide of iron; and the burrows, which the worms made through this sand, were lined or coated in the usual manner with their castings, formed of the sand mingled with their intestinal secretions and the refuse of the digested leaves; and this sand had almost wholly lost its red colour. When small portions of it were placed under the microscope, most of the grains were seen to be transparent and colourless, owing to the dissolution of the oxide; whilst almost all the grains taken from other parts of the pot were coated with the oxide. Acetic acid produced hardly any effect on this sand; and even hydrochloric, nitric and sulphuric acids, diluted as in the Pharmacopœia, produced less effect than did the acids in the intestines of the worms.

Mr. A. A. Julien has lately collected all the extant information about the acids generated in humus, which, according to some chemists, amount to more than a dozen different kinds. These acids, as well as their acid salts (i.e., in combination with potash, soda, and ammonia), act energetically on

carbonate of lime and on the oxides of iron.
It is, also, known that some of these acids,
which were called long ago by Thénard azo-
humic, are enabled to dissolve colloid silica in
proportion to the nitrogen which they contain.[*]
In the formation of these latter acids worms
probably afford some aid, for Dr. H. Johnson
informs me that by Nessler's test he found
0·018 per cent. of ammonia in their castings.

The several humus-acids, which appear, as
we have just seen, to be generated within the
bodies of worms during the digestive process,
and their acid salts, play a highly important
part, according to the recent observations of
Mr. Julien, in the disintegration of various
kinds of rocks.   It has long been known that
the carbonic acid, and no doubt nitric and
nitrous acids, which are present in rain-water,
act in like manner.   There is, also, a great
excess of carbonic acid in all soils, especially
in rich soils, and this is dissolved by the water

* A. A. Julien "On the Geological action of the Humus-acids,"
'Proc. American Assoc. Science,' vol. xxviii., 1879, p. 311.
Also on "Chemical erosion on Mountain Summits;" 'New York
Academy of Sciences,' Oct. 14, 1878, as quoted in the 'American
Naturalist.' See also, on this subject, S. W. Johnson, "How
Crops Feed," 1870, p. 138.

in the ground.   The living roots of plants,
moreover, as Sachs and others have shown,
quickly corrode and leave their impressions
on polished slabs of marble, dolomite and
phosphate of lime.   They will attack even
basalt and sandstone.*   But we are not here
concerned with agencies which are wholly
independent of the action of worms.

The combination of any acid with a base
is much facilitated by agitation, as fresh
surfaces are thus continually brought into
contact.   This will be thoroughly effected
with the particles of stone and earth in the
intestines of worms, during the digestive process; and it should be remembered that the
entire mass of the mould over every field,
passes, in the course of a few years, through
their alimentary canals.   Moreover as the old
burrows slowly collapse, and as fresh castings
are continually brought to the surface, the
whole superficial layer of mould slowly re-
volves or circulates; and the friction of the
particles one with another will rub off the
finest films of disintegrated matter as soon as

* See, for references on this subject, S. W. Johnson, "How
Crops Feed," 1870, p. 326.

they are formed. Through these several
means, minute fragments of rocks of many
kinds and mere particles in the soil will be
continually exposed to chemical decomposition; and thus the amount of soil will tend
to increase.

As worms line their burrows with their
castings, and as the burrows penetrate to a
depth of 5 or 6, or even more feet, some
small amount of the humus-acids will be
carried far down, and will there act on the
underlying rocks and fragments of rock.
Thus the thickness of the soil, if none be removed from the surface, will steadily though
slowly tend to increase; but the accumulation
will after a time delay the disintegration of
the underlying rocks and of the more deeply
seated particles. For the humus-acids which
are generated chiefly in the upper layer of
vegetable mould, are extremely unstable com-
pounds, and are liable to decomposition before
they reach any considerable depth.* A thick
bed of overlying soil will also check the
downward extension of great fluctuations of
temperature, and in cold countries will check

* This statement is taken from Mr. Julien, 'Proc. American
Assoc. Science,' vol. xxviii., 1879. p. 330.

the powerful action of frost.   The free access
of air will likewise be excluded.   From these
several causes disintegration would be almost
arrested, if the overlying mould were to
increase much in thickness, owing to none or
little being removed from the surface.*   In
my own immediate neighbourhood we have a
curious proof how effectually a few feet of
clay checks some change which goes on in
flints, lying freely exposed;   for the large
ones which have lain for some time on the
surface of ploughed fields cannot be used for
building; they will not cleave properly and
are said by the workmen to be rotten.†   It is

* The preservative power of a layer of mould and turf is often
shown by the perfect state of the glacial scratches on rocks when
first uncovered.   Mr. J. Geikie maintains, in his last very interesting work ('Prehistoric Europe,' 1881), that the more perfect
scratches are probably due to the last access of cold and increase
of ice, during the long-continued, intermittent glacial period.

† Many geologists have felt much surprise at the complete
disappearance of flints over wide and nearly level areas, from
which the chalk has been removed by subaerial denudation.
But the surface of every flint is coated by an opaque modified
layer, which will just yield to a steel point, whilst the freshly-
fractured, translucent surface will not thus yield.   The removal by atmospheric agencies of the outer modified surfaces
of freely exposed flints, though no doubt excessively slow, together with the modification travelling inwards, will, as may be
suspected, ultimately lead to their complete disintegration, notwithstanding that they appear to be so extremely durable.

therefore necessary to obtain flints for building purposes from the bed of red clay overlying the chalk (the residue of its dissolution
by rainwater) or from the chalk itself.

Not only do worms aid indirectly in the
chemical disintegration of rocks, but there is
good reason to believe that they likewise act
in a direct and mechanical manner on the
smaller particles. All the species which
swallow earth are furnished with gizzards;
and these are lined with so thick a chitinous
membrane, that Perrier speaks of it,* as " une
véritable armature." The gizzard is surrounded by powerful transverse muscles,
which, according to Claparède, are about ten
times as thick as the longitudinal ones; and
Perrier saw them contracting energetically.
Worms belonging to one genus, Digaster,
have two distinct but quite similar gizzards;
and in another genus, Moniligaster, the
second gizzard consists of four pouches, one
succeeding the other, so that it may almost
be said to have five gizzards.†   In the same

* 'Archives de Zoolog. expér.' tom. iii. 1874, p. 409.
† 'Nouvelles Archives du Muséum,' tom. viii. 1872, p. 95,
131.

manner as gallinaceous and struthious birds swallow stones to aid in the trituration of their food, so it appears to be with terricolous worms. The gizzards of thirty-eight of our common worms were opened, and in twenty-five of them small stones or grains of sand, sometimes together with the hard calcareous concretions formed within the anterior calciferous glands, were found, and in two others concretions alone. In the gizzards · of the remaining worms there were no stones; but some of these were not real exceptions, as the gizzards were opened late in the autumn, when the worms had ceased to feed and their gizzards were quite empty.*

When worms make their burrows through earth abounding with little stones, no doubt many will be unavoidably swallowed; but it must not be supposed that this fact accounts for the frequency with which stones and sand are found in their gizzards. For beads of glass and fragments of brick and of hard tiles were scattered over the surface

* Morren, in speaking of the earth in the alimentary canals of worms, says, "præsepè cum lapillis commixtam vidi:" 'De umbrici terrestris,' &c., 1829, p. 16.

of the earth, in pots in which worms were kept and had already made their burrows; and very many of these beads and fragments were picked up and swallowed by the worms, for they were found in their castings, intestines, and gizzards. They even swallowed the coarse red dust, formed by the pounding of the tiles. Nor can it be supposed that they mistook the beads and fragments for food; for we have seen that their taste is delicate enough to distinguish between different kinds of leaves. It is therefore manifest that they swallow hard objects, such as bits of stone, beads of glass and angular fragments of bricks or tiles for some special purpose; and it can hardly be doubted that this is to aid their gizzards in crushing and grinding the earth, which they so largely consume. That such hard objects are not necessary for crushing leaves, may be inferred from the fact that certain species, which live in mud or water and feed on dead or living vegetable matter, but which do not swallow earth, are not provided with gizzards,[*] and

* Perrier, 'Archives de Zoolog. expér.' tom. iii. 1874, p. 419.

therefore cannot have the power of utilising stones.

During the grinding process, the particles of earth must be rubbed against one another, and between the stones and the tough lining membrane of the gizzard. The softer particles will thus suffer some attrition, and will perhaps even be crushed. This conclusion is supported by the appearance of freshly ejected castings, for these often reminded me of the appearance of paint which has just been ground by a workman between two flat stones. Morren remarks that the intestinal canal is "impleta tenuissimâ terrâ, veluti in pulverem redactâ." [*] Perrier also speaks of " l'état de pâte excessivement fine à laquelle est réduite la terre qu'ils rejettent," &c.[†]

As the amount of trituration which the particles of earth undergo in the gizzards of worms possesses some interest (as we shall hereafter see), I endeavoured to obtain evidence on this head by carefully examining many of the fragments which had passed

[*] Morren, ' De Lumbrici terrestris,' &c., p. 16.
[†] ' Archives de Zoolog. Expér.' tom. iii. 1874, p. 418.

through their alimentary canals. With worms living in a state of nature, it is of course impossible to know how much the fragments may have been worn before they were swallowed. It is, however, clear that worms do not habitually select already rounded particles, for sharply angular bits of flint and of other hard rocks were often found in their gizzards or intestines. On three occasions sharp spines from the stems of rose-bushes were thus found. Worms kept in confinement repeatedly swallowed angular fragments of hard tile, coal, cinders, and even the sharpest fragments of glass. Gallinaceous and struthious birds retain the same stones in their gizzards for a long time, which thus become well rounded; but this does not appear to be the case with worms, judging from the large number of the fragments of tiles, glass beads, stones, &c., commonly found in their castings and intestines. So that unless the same fragments were to pass repeatedly through their gizzards, visible signs of attrition in the fragments could hardly be expected, except perhaps in the case of very soft stones.

I will now give such evidence of attrition
as I have been able to collect. In the
gizzards of some worms dug out of a thin bed
of mould over the chalk, there were many well-
rounded small fragments of chalk, and two
fragments of the shells of a land-mollusc (as
ascertained by their microscopical structure),
which latter were not only rounded but
somewhat polished. The calcareous concretions formed in the calciferous glands, which
are often found in their gizzards, intestines,
and occasionally in their castings, when of
large size, sometimes appeared to have been
rounded; but with all calcareous bodies
the rounded appearance may be partly or
wholly due to their corrosion by carbonic
acid and the humus-acids. In the gizzards
of several worms collected in my kitchen
garden near a hothouse, eight little fragments of cinders were found, and of these,
six appeared more or less rounded, as were
two bits of brick; but some other bits were
not at all rounded. A farm-road near
Abinger Hall had been covered seven years
before with brick-rubbish to the depth of
about 6 inches; turf had grown over this

rubbish on both sides of the road for a width of 18 inches, and on this turf there were innumerable castings. Some of them were coloured of a uniform red owing to the presence of much brick-dust, and they contained many particles of brick and of hard mortar from 1 to 3 mm. in diameter, most of which were plainly rounded; but all these particles may have been rounded before they were protected by the turf and were swallowed, like those on the bare parts of the road which were much worn. A hole in a pasture-field had been filled up with brick-rubbish at the same time, viz., seven years ago, and was now covered with turf; and here the castings contained very many particles of brick, all more or less rounded; and this brick-rubbish, after being shot into the hole, could not have undergone any attrition. Again, old bricks very little broken, together with fragments of mortar, were laid down to form walks, and were then covered with from 4 to 6 inches of gravel; six little fragments of brick were extracted from castings collected on these walks, three of which were plainly worn.

There were also very many particles of hard mortar, about half of which were well rounded; and it is not credible that these could have suffered so much corrosion from the action of carbonic acid in the course of only seven years.

Much better evidence of the attrition of hard objects in the gizzards of worms, is afforded by the state of the small fragments of tiles or bricks, and of concrete in the castings thrown up where ancient buildings once stood. As all the mould covering a field passes every few years through the bodies of worms, the same small fragments will probably be swallowed and brought to the surface many times in the course of centuries. It should be premised that in the several following cases, the finer matter was first washed away from the castings, and then *all* the particles of bricks, tiles and concrete were collected without any selection, and were afterwards examined. Now in the castings ejected between the tesserae on one of the buried floors of the Roman villa at Abinger, there were many particles (from $\frac{1}{2}$ to 2 mm. in diameter) of tiles and concrete, which it

was impossible to look at with the naked eye
or through a strong lens, and doubt for a
moment that they had almost all undergone
much attrition. I speak thus after having
examined small water-worn pebbles, formed
from Roman bricks, which M. Henri de
Saussure had the kindness to send me, and
which he had extracted from sand and gravel
beds, deposited on the shores of the Lake of
Geneva, at a former period when the water
stood at about two metres above its present
level. The smallest of these water-worn
pebbles of brick from Geneva resembled
closely many of those extracted from the
gizzards of worms, but the larger ones were
somewhat smoother.

Four castings found on the recently uncovered, tesselated floor of the great room in
the Roman villa at Brading, contained many
particles of tile or brick, of mortar, and of
hard white cement; and the majority of these
appeared plainly worn. The particles of
mortar, however, seemed to have suffered
more corrosion than attrition, for grains of
silex often projected from their surfaces.
Castings from within the nave of Beaulieu

Abbey, which was destroyed by Henry VIII., were collected from a level expanse of turf, overlying the buried tesselated pavement, through which worm-burrows passed; and these castings contained innumerable particles of tiles and bricks, of concrete and cement, the majority of which had manifestly undergone some or much attrition. There were also many minute flakes of a micaceous slate, the points of which were rounded. If the above supposition, that in all these cases the same minute fragments have passed several times through the gizzards of worms, be rejected, notwithstanding its inherent probability, we must then assume that in all the above cases the many rounded fragments found in the castings had all accidentally undergone much attrition before they were swallowed; and this is highly improbable.

On the other hand it must be stated that fragments of ornamental tiles, somewhat harder than common tiles or bricks, which had been swallowed only once by worms kept in confinement, were with the doubtful exception of one or two of the smallest grains, not at all rounded. Nevertheless some of them appeared a little worn, though not rounded. Notwithstanding these cases, if we consider the evidence above given, there can be little doubt that the fragments, which serve as millstones in the gizzards of worms, suffer, when of a not very hard texture, some amount of attrition; and that the smaller particles in the earth, which is habitually swallowed in such astonishingly large quantities by worms, are ground together and are thus levigated. If this be the case, the " terra tenuissima,"— the "pâte excessivement fine,"—of which the castings largely consist, is in part due to the mechanical action of the gizzard;* and this fine matter, as we shall see in the next chapter, is that which is chiefly washed away from the innumerable castings on every field during each heavy shower of rain. If the softer stones yield at all, the harder ones will suffer some slight amount of wear and tear.   .

* This conclusion reminds me of the vast amount of extremely fine chalky mud which is found within the lagoons of many atolls, where the sea is tranquil and waves cannot triturate the blocks of coral. This mud must, as I believe (' The Structure and Distribution of Coral-Reefs,' 2nd edit. 1874, p. 19), be attributed to the innumerable annelids and other animals which burrow into the dead coral, and to the fishes, Holothurians, &c., which browse on the living corals.

The trituration of small particles of stone in the gizzards ·of worms is of more importance under a geological point of view than may at first appear to be the case ; for Mr. Sorby has clearly shown that the ordinary means of disintegration, namely running water and the waves of the sea, act with less and less power on fragments of rock the smaller they are. "Hence," as he remarks, "even making no allowance for the extra "buoying up of very minute particles by a "current of water, depending on surface "cohesion, the effects of wearing on the form "of the grains must vary directly as their "diameter or thereabouts. If so, a grain $\frac{1}{10}$ "of an inch in diameter would be worn ten "times as much as one $\frac{1}{100}$ of an inch in "diameter, and at least a hundred times as "much as one $\frac{1}{1000}$ of an inch in diameter. "Perhaps, then, we may conclude that a "grain $\frac{1}{10}$ of an inch in diameter would be "worn as much or more in drifting a mile as "a grain $\frac{1}{1000}$ of an inch in being drifted "100 miles. On the same principle a pebble "one inch in diameter would be worn re- "latively more by being drifted only a few

" hundred yards."*   Nor should we forget, in considering the power which worms exert in triturating particles of rock, that there is good evidence that on each acre of land, which is sufficiently damp and not too sandy, gravelly or rocky for worms to inhabit, a weight of more than ten tons of earth annually passes through their bodies and is brought to the surface.   The result for a country of the size of Great Britain, within a period not very long in a geological sense, such as a million years, cannot be insignificant; for the ten tons of earth has to be multiplied first by the above number of years, and then by the number of acres fully stocked with worms; and in England, together with Scotland, the land which is cultivated and is well fitted for these animals, has been estimated at above 32 million acres.   The product is 320 million million tons of earth.

* Anniversary Address: 'The Quarterly Journal of the Geological Soc.' May 1880, p. 59.

CHAPTER VI.

THE DENUDATION OF THE LAND—*continued.*

Denudation aided by recently ejected castings flowing down inclined grass-covered surfaces—The amount of earth which annually flows downwards—The effect of tropical rain on worm castings—The finest particles of earth washed completely away from castings—The disintegration of dried castings into pellets, and their rolling down inclined surfaces—The formation of little ledges on hill-sides, in part due to the accumulation of disintegrated castings—Castings blown to leeward over level land—An attempt to estimate the amount thus blown—The degradation of ancient encampments and tumuli—The preservation of the crowns and furrows on land anciently ploughed—The formation and amount of mould over the Chalk formation.

WE are now prepared to consider the more direct part which worms take in the denudation of the land. When reflecting on sub-aerial denudation, it formerly appeared to me, as it has to others, that a nearly level or very gently inclined surface, covered with turf, could suffer no loss during even a long lapse of time. It may, however, be urged that at long intervals, debacles of rain or

water-spouts would remove all the mould
from a very gentle slope; but when examining the steep, turf-covered slopes in
Glen Roy, I was struck with the fact how
rarely any such event could have happened
since the Glacial period, as was plain from the
well-preserved state of the three successive
" roads " or lake-margins. But the difficulty
in believing that earth in any appreciable
quantity can be removed from a gently inclined surface, covered with vegetation and
matted with roots, is removed through the
agency of worms. For the many castings
which are thrown up during rain, and those
thrown up some little time before heavy rain,
flow for a short distance down an inclined
surface. Moreover much of the finest levigated earth is washed completely away from
the castings. During dry weather castings
often disintegrate into small rounded pellets,
and these from their weight often roll down
any slope. This is more especially apt to
occur when they are started by the wind,
and probably when started by the touch of an
animal, however small. We shall also see
that a strong wind blows all the castings,

even on a level field, to leeward, whilst they are soft; and in like manner the pellets when they are dry. If the wind blows in nearly the direction of an inclined surface, the flowing down of the castings is much aided.

The observations on which these several statements are founded must now be given in some detail. Castings when first ejected are viscid and soft; during rain, at which time worms apparently prefer to eject them, they are still softer; so that I have sometimes thought that worms must swallow much water at such times. However this may be, rain, even when not very heavy, if long continued, renders recently-ejected castings semi-fluid; and on level ground they then spread out into thin, circular, flat discs, exactly as would so much honey or very soft mortar, with all traces of their vermiform structure lost. This latter fact was sometimes made evident, when a worm had subsequently bored through a flat circular disc of this kind, and heaped up a fresh vermiform mass in the centre. These flat subsided discs have been repeatedly seen by me after heavy rain, in many places on land of all kinds.

On the flowing of wet castings, and the rolling of dry disintegrated castings down inclined surfaces.—When castings are ejected on an inclined surface during or shortly before heavy rain, they cannot fail to flow a little down the slope. Thus, on some steep slopes in Knowle Park, which were covered with coarse grass and had apparently existed in this state from time immemorial, I found (Oct. 22, 1872) after several wet days that almost all the many castings were considerably elongated in the line of the slope; and that they now consisted of smooth, only slightly conical masses. Whenever the mouths of the burrows could be found from which the earth had been ejected, there was more earth below than above them. After some heavy storms of rain (Jan. 25, 1872) two rather steeply inclined fields near Down, which had formerly been ploughed and were now rather sparsely clothed with poor grass, were visited, and many castings extended down the slopes for a length of 5 inches, which was twice or thrice the usual diameter

of the castings thrown up on the level parts
of these same fields.   On some fine grassy
slopes in Holwood Park, inclined at angles
between 8° and 11° 30' with the horizon,
where the surface apparently had never been
disturbed by the hand of man, castings
abounded in extraordinary numbers; and a
space 16 inches in length transversely to the
slope and 6 inches in the line of the slope,
was completely coated, between the blades of
grass, with a uniform sheet of confluent and
subsided castings.   Here also in many places
the castings had flowed down the slope, and
now formed smooth narrow patches of earth,
6, 7, and 7½ inches in length.   Some of these
consisted of two castings, one above the other,
which had become so completely confluent
that they could hardly be distinguished.   On
my lawn, clothed with very fine grass, most
of the castings are black, but some are
yellowish from earth having been brought
up from a greater depth than usual, and the
flowing-down of these yellow castings after
heavy rain, could be clearly seen where the
slope was 5°; and where it was less than 1°
some evidence of their flowing down could
18

still be detected. On another occasion, after rain which was never heavy, but which lasted for 18 hours, all the castings on this same gently inclined lawn had lost their vermiform structure; and they had flowed, so that fully two-thirds of the ejected earth lay below the mouths of the burrows.

These observations led me to make others with more care. Eight castings were found on my lawn, where the grass-blades are fine and close together, and three others on a field with coarse grass. The inclination of the surface at the eleven places where these castings were collected varied between 4° 30' and 17° 30'; the mean of the eleven inclinations being 9° 26'. The length of the castings in the direction of the slope was first measured with as much accuracy as their irregularities would permit. It was found possible to make these measurements within about $\frac{1}{8}$ of an inch, but one of the castings was too irregular to admit of measurement. The average length in the direction of the slope of the remaining ten castings was 2·03 inches. The castings were then divided with a knife into two parts along a horizontal line passing through the mouth of the burrow, which was discovered by slicing off the turf; and all the ejected earth was separately collected, namely the part above the hole and the part below. Afterwards these two parts were weighed. In every case there was much more earth below than above; the mean weight of that above being 103 grains, and of that below 205 grains; so that the latter was very nearly double the former. As on level ground castings are commonly thrown up almost equally round the mouths of the burrows, this difference in weight indicates the amount of ejected earth which had flowed down the slope. But very many more observations would be requisite to arrive at any general result; for the nature of the vegetation and other accidental circumstances, such as the heaviness of the rain, the direction and force of the wind, &c., appear to be more important in determining the quantity of the earth which flows down a slope than its angle. Thus with four castings on my lawn (included in the above eleven) where the mean slope was 7° 19', the difference in the amount of earth above and below the burrows was greater than with three other castings on the same lawn where the mean slope was 12° 5′.

We may, however, take the above eleven cases, which are accurate as far as they go, and calculate the weight of the ejected earth which annually flows down a slope having a mean inclination of 9° 26′. This was done by my son George. It has been shown that almost exactly two-thirds of the ejected earth is found below the mouth of the burrow and one-third above it. Now if the two-thirds which is below the hole be divided into two equal parts, the upper half of this two-thirds exactly counterbalances the one-third which is above the hole, so that as far as regards the one-third above and the upper half of the two-thirds below, there is no flow of earth down the hill-side. The earth constituting the lower half of the two-thirds is, however, displaced through distances which are different for every part of it, but which may be represented by the distance between the middle point of the lower half of the two-thirds and the hole. So that the average distance of displacement is a half of the whole length of the worm-casting. Now the

average length of ten out of the above
eleven castings was 2·03 inches, and half of
this we may take as being one inch. It may
therefore be concluded that one-third of the
whole earth brought to the surface was in
these cases carried down the slope through
one inch.

It was shown in the third chapter that on
Leith Hill Common, dry earth weighing at
least 7·453 lbs. was brought up by worms to
the surface on a square yard in the course of
a year. If a square yard be drawn on a
hill-side with two of its sides horizontal, then
it is clear that only $\frac{1}{36}$ part of the earth
brought up on that square yard would be
near enough to its lower side to cross it,
supposing the displacement of the earth to
be through one inch. But it appears that
only $\frac{1}{3}$ of the earth brought up can be considered to flow downwards; hence $\frac{1}{3}$ of $\frac{1}{36}$ or
$\frac{1}{108}$ of 7·453 lbs. will cross the lower side of
our square yard in a year. Now $\frac{1}{108}$ of
7·453 lbs. is 1·1 oz. Therefore 1·1 oz. of dry
earth will annually cross each linear yard running horizontally along a slope having the
above inclination; or very nearly 7 lbs. will

annually cross a horizontal line, 100 yards in length, on a hill-side having this inclination.

A more accurate, though still very rough, calculation can be made of the bulk of earth, which in its natural damp state annually flows down the same slope over a yard-line drawn horizontally across it. From the several cases given in the third chapter, it is known that the castings annually brought to the surface on a square yard, if uniformly spread out would form a layer ·2 of an inch in thickness: it therefore follows by a calculation similar to the one already given, that $\frac{1}{3}$ of ·2 × 36, or 2·4 cubic inches of damp earth will annually cross a horizontal line one yard in length on a hill-side with the above inclination. This bulk of damp castings was found to weigh 1·85 oz. Therefore 11·56 lbs. of damp earth instead of 7 lbs. of dry earth as by the former calculation, would annually cross a line 100 yards in length on our inclined surface.

In these calculations it has been assumed that the castings flow a short distance downwards during the whole year, but this occurs only with those ejected during or shortly before rain; so that the above results are thus far exaggerated. On the other hand, during rain much of the finest earth is washed to a considerable distance from the castings, even where the slope is an extremely gentle one, and is thus wholly lost as far as the above calculations are concerned. Castings ejected during dry weather and which have set hard, lose in the same manner a considerable quantity of fine earth. Dried castings, moreover, are apt to disintegrate into little pellets, which often roll or are blown down any inclined surface. Therefore the above result, namely that 2·4 cubic inches of earth (weighing 1·85 oz. whilst damp) annually crosses a yard-line of the specified kind, is probably not much if at all exaggerated.

This amount is small; but we should bear in mind how many branching valleys intersect most countries, the whole length of which must be very great; and that earth is steadily travelling down both turf-covered sides of each valley. For every 100 yards in length in a valley with sides sloping as in the foregoing cases, 480 cubic inches of damp earth, weighing above 23 pounds, will annually reach the bottom. Here a thick bed of alluvium will accumulate, ready to be washed away in the course of centuries, as the stream in the middle meanders from side to side.

If it could be shown that worms generally excavate their burrows at right angles to an inclined surface, and this would be their shortest course for bringing up earth from beneath, then as the old burrows collapsed from the weight of the superincumbent soil, the collapsing would inevitably cause the whole bed of vegetable mould to sink or slide slowly down the inclined surface. But to ascertain the direction of many burrows was found too difficult and troublesome. A straight piece of wire was, however, pushed into twenty-five burrows on several sloping fields, and in eight cases the burrows were nearly at right angles to the slope; whilst in the remaining cases they were indifferently directed at various angles, either upwards or downwards with respect to the slope.

In countries where the rain is very heavy,

as in the tropics, the castings appear, as
might have been expected, to be washed
down in a greater degree than in England.
Mr. Scott informs me that near Calcutta the
tall columnar castings (previously described).
the diameter of which is usually between 1
and 1½ inch, subside on a level surface,
after heavy rain, into almost circular, thin,
flat discs, between 3 and 4 and sometimes 5
inches in diameter. Three fresh castings,
which had been ejected in the Botanic
Gardens "on a slightly inclined, grass-
" covered, artificial bank of loamy clay," were
carefully measured, and had a mean height
of 2·17, and a mean diameter of 1·43 inches;
these after heavy rain, formed elongated
patches of earth, with a mean length in the
direction of the slope of 5·83 inches. As the
earth had spread very little up the slope, a
large part, judging from the original diameter
of these castings, must have flowed bodily
downwards about 4 inches. Moreover some
of the finest earth of which they were composed must have been washed completely
away to a still greater distance. In drier
sites near Calcutta, a species of worm ejects

its castings, not in vermiform masses, but in little pellets of varying sizes : these are very numerous in some places, and Mr. Scott says that they " are washed away by every " shower."

I was led to believe that a considerable quantity of fine earth is washed quite away from castings during rain, from the surfaces of old ones being often studded with coarse particles. Accordingly a little fine precipitated chalk, moistened with saliva or gumwater, so as to be slightly viscid and of the same consistence as a fresh casting, was placed on the summits of several castings and gently mixed with them. These castings were then watered through a very fine rose, the drops from which were closer together than those of rain, but not nearly so large as those in a thunder storm ; nor did they strike the ground with nearly so much force as drops during heavy rain. A casting thus treated · subsided with surprising slowness, owing as I suppose to its viscidity. It did not flow bodily down the grass-covered surface of the lawn, which was here inclined at an angle of 16° 20'; nevertheless many par-

ticles of the chalk were found three inches
below the casting. The experiment was repeated on three other castings on different
parts of the lawn, which sloped at 2° 30′,
3° and 6°; and particles of chalk could be
seen between 4 and 5 inches below the casting; and after the surface had become dry,
particles were found in two cases at a distance
of 5 and 6 inches. Several other castings
with precipitated chalk placed on their
summits were left to the natural action of
the rain. In one case, after rain which was
not heavy, the casting was longitudinally
streaked with white. In two other cases the
surface of the ground was rendered somewhat white for a distance of one inch from
the casting; and some soil collected at a distance of $2\frac{1}{2}$ inches, where the slope was 7°,
effervesced slightly when placed in acid.
After one or two weeks, the chalk was wholly
or almost wholly washed away from all the
castings on which it had been placed, and
these had recovered their natural colour.

It may be here remarked that after very
heavy rain shallow pools may be seen on level
or nearly level fields, where the soil is not

very porous, and the water in them is often
slightly muddy; when such little pools have
dried, the leaves and blades of grass at their
bottoms are generally coated with a thin layer
of mud. This mud I believe is derived in
large part from recently ejected castings.

Dr. King informs me that the majority of
the before described gigantic castings, which
he found on a fully exposed, bare, gravelly
knoll on the Nilgiri Mountains in India, had
been more or less weathered by the previous
north-east monsoon; and most of them presented a subsided appearance. The worms
here eject their castings only during the rainy
season; and at the time of Dr. King's visit no
rain had fallen for 110 days. He carefully
examined the ground between the place
where these huge castings lay, and a little
water-course at the base of the knoll, and
nowhere was there any accumulation of fine
earth, such as would necessarily have been
left by the disintegration of the castings if
they had not been wholly removed. He
therefore has no hesitation in asserting that
the whole of these huge castings are annually
washed during the two monsoons (when

about 100 inches of rain fall) into the little
water-course, and thence into the plains
lying below at a depth of 3000 or 4000 feet.

Castings ejected before or during dry
weather become hard, sometimes surprisingly
hard, from the particles of earth having been
cemented together by the intestinal secretions. Frost seems to be less effective in
their disintegration than might have been
expected. Nevertheless they readily disintegrate into small pellets, after being alternately moistened with rain and again dried.
Those which have flowed during rain down a
slope, disintegrate in the same manner. Such
pellets often roll a little down any sloping
surface; their descent being sometimes much
aided by the wind. The whole bottom of a
broad dry ditch in my grounds, where there
were very few fresh castings, was completely
covered with these pellets or disintegrated
castings, which had rolled down the steep
sides, inclined at an angle of 27°.

Near Nice, in places where the great cylindrical castings, previously described, abound,
the soil consists of very fine arenaceo-cal-
careous loam; and Dr. King informs me that

these castings are extremely liable to crumble
during dry weather into small fragments,
which are soon acted on by rain, and then
sink down so as to be no longer distinguishable from the surrounding soil.   He sent me
a mass of such disintegrated castings, collected
on the top of a bank, where none could have
rolled down from above.   They must have
been ejected within the previous five or six
months, but they now consisted of more or less
rounded fragments of all sizes, from $\frac{3}{4}$ of an
inch in diameter to minute grains and mere
dust.   Dr. King witnessed the crumbling
process whilst drying some perfect castings,
which he afterwards sent me.   Mr. Scott also
remarks on the crumbling of the castings
near Calcutta and on the mountains of
Sikkim during the hot and dry season.

When the castings near Nice had been
ejected on an inclined surface, the disintegrated fragments rolled downwards, without
losing their distinctive shape; and in some
places could " be collected in basketfuls."   Dr.
King observed a striking instance of this fact
on the Corniche road, where a drain, about
$2\frac{1}{2}$ feet wide and 9 inches deep, had been made

to catch the surface drainage from the adjoining hill-side. The bottom of this drain was covered for a distance of several hundred yards, to a depth of from $1\frac{1}{2}$ to 3 inches, by a layer of broken castings, still retaining their characteristic shape. Nearly all these innumerable fragments had rolled down from above, for extremely few castings had been ejected in the drain itself. The hill-side was steep, but varied much in inclination, which Dr. King estimated at from 30° to 60° with the horizon. He climbed up the slope, and "found every here and there little embank- "ments, formed by fragments of the castings "that had been arrested in their downward "progress by irregularities of the surface, "by stones, twigs, &c. One little group of "plants of *Anemone hortensis* had acted in this "manner, and quite a small bank of soil had "collected round it. Much of this soil had "crumbled down, but a great deal of it still "retained the form of castings." Dr. King dug up this plant, and was struck with the thickness of the soil which must have recently accumulated over the crown of the rhizoma, as shown by the length of the bleached petioles, in comparison with those of other plants of the same kind, where there had been no such accumulation. The earth thus accumulated had no doubt been secured (as I have everywhere seen) by the smaller roots of the plants. After describing this and other analogous cases, Dr. King concludes : " I can have no doubt that worms " help greatly in the process of denudation."

Ledges of earth on steep hill-sides.—Little horizontal ledges, one above another, have been observed on steep grassy slopes in many parts of the world. Their formation has been attributed to animals travelling repeatedly along the slope in the same horizontal lines while grazing, and that they do thus move and use the ledges is certain ; but Professor Henslow (a most careful observer) told Sir J. Hooker that he was convinced that this was not the sole cause of their formation. Sir J. Hooker saw such ledges on the Himalayan and Atlas ranges, where there were no domesticated animals and not many wild ones ; but these latter would, it is probable, use the ledges at night while grazing like our domesticated animals. A friend observed for me the ledges on the Alps of Switzerland, and states that they ran at 3 or 4 ft. one above the other and were about a foot in breadth. They had been deeply pitted by the feet of grazing cows. Similar ledges were observed by the same friend on our Chalk downs, and on an old talus of chalk-fragments (thrown out of a quarry) which had become clothed with turf.

My son Francis examined a Chalk escarpment near Lewes; and here on a part which was very steep, sloping at 40° with the horizon, about 30 flat ledges extended horizontally for more than 100 yards, at an average distance of about 20 inches, one beneath the other. They were from 9 to 10 inches in breadth. When viewed from a distance they presented a striking appearance, owing to their parallelism; but when examined closely, they were seen to be somewhat sinuous, and one often ran into another, giving the appearance of one ledge having forked into two. They are formed of light-coloured earth, which on the outside, where thickest, was in one case 9 inches, and in another case between 6 and 7 inches in thickness. Above the ledges, the thickness of the earth over the chalk was in

19

the former case 4 and in the latter only 3 inches. The grass grew more vigorously on the outer edges of the ledges than on any other part of the slope, and here formed a tufted fringe. Their middle part was bare, but whether this had been caused by the trampling of sheep, which sometimes frequent the ledges, my son could not ascertain. Nor could he feel sure how much of the earth on the middle and bare parts, consisted of disintegrated worm-castings which had rolled down from above; but he felt convinced that some had thus originated; and it was manifest that the ledges with their grass-fringed edges would arrest any small object rolling down from above.

At one end or side of the oank bearing these ledges, the surface consisted in parts of bare chalk, and here the ledges were very irregular. At the other end of the bank, the slope suddenly became less steep, and here the ledges ceased rather abruptly; but little embankments only a foot or two in length were still present. The slope became steeper lower down the hill, and the regular ledges then reappeared. Another of my sons observed, on

the inland side of Beachy Head, where the
surface sloped at about 25°, many short little
embankments like those just mentioned.
They extended horizontally and were from a
few inches to two or three feet in length.
They supported tufts of grass growing
vigorously. The average thickness of the
mould of which they were formed, taken
from nine measurements, was 4·5 inches;
while that of the mould above and beneath
them was on an average only 3·2 inches, and
on each side, on the same level, 3·1 inches.
On the upper parts of the slope, these embankments showed no signs of having been
trampled on by sheep, but in the lower parts
such signs were fairly plain. No long continuous ledges had here been formed.

If the little embankments above the Corniche road, which Dr. King saw in the act
of formation by the accumulation of disintegrated and rolled worm-castings, were to
become confluent along horizontal lines, ledges
would be formed. Each embankment would
tend to extend laterally by the lateral extension
of the arrested castings; and animals grazing on
a steep slope would almost certainly make use

of every prominence at nearly the same level, and would indent the turf between them ; and such intermediate indentations would again arrest the castings.   An irregular ledge when once formed would also tend to become more regular and horizontal by some of the castings rolling laterally from the higher to the lower parts, which would thus be raised.   Any projection beneath a ledge would not afterwards receive distintegrated matter from above, and would tend to be obliterated by rain and other atmospheric agencies.   There is some analogy between the formation, as here supposed, of these ledges, and that of the ripples of wind-drifted sand as described by Lyell.*

The steep, grass-covered sides of a mountainous valley in Westmoreland, called Grisedale, was marked in many places with innumerable, almost horizontal, little ledges, or rather lines of miniature cliffs.   Their formation was in no way connected with the action of worms, for castings could not anywhere be seen (and their absence is an inexplicable fact) although the turf lay in many places over a considerable thickness of

* 'Elements of Geology,' 1865, p. 20

boulder-clay and moraine rubbish. Nor, as far as I could judge, was the formation of these little cliffs at all closely connected with the trampling of cows or sheep. It appeared as if the whole superficial, somewhat argillaceous earth, while partially held together by the roots of the grasses, had slided a little way down the mountain sides; and in thus sliding, had yielded and cracked in horizontal lines, transversely to the slope.

Castings blown to leeward by the wind.—We have seen that moist castings flow, and that disintegrated castings roll down any inclined surface; and we shall now see that castings, recently ejected on level grass-covered surfaces, are blown during gales of wind accompanied by rain to leeward. This has been observed by me many times on many fields during several successive years. After such gales, the castings present a gently inclined and smooth, or sometimes furrowed, surface to windward, while they are steeply inclined or precipitous to leeward, so that they resemble on a miniature scale glacier-ground hillocks of rock. They are often cavernous on the leeward side, from the upper part having curled over the lower part. During one unusually heavy south-west gale with torrents of rain, many castings were wholly blown to leeward, so that the mouths of the burrows were left naked and exposed on the windward side. Recent castings naturally flow down an inclined surface, but on a grassy field, which sloped between 10° and 15°, several were found after a heavy gale blown up the slope. This likewise occurred on another occasion on a part of my lawn where the slope was somewhat less. On a third occasion, the castings on the steep, grass-covered sides of a valley, down which a gale had blown, were directed obliquely instead of straight down the slope; and this was obviously due to the combined action of the wind and gravity. Four castings on my lawn, where the downward inclination was 0° 45′, 1°, 3° and 3° 30′ (mean 2° 45′) towards the north-east, after a heavy south-west gale with rain, were divided across the mouths of the burrows and weighed in the manner formerly described. The mean weight of the earth below the mouths of burrows and to leeward, was to that above the mouths and on the windward side as 2¾ to 1; whereas we have seen that with several castings which had flowed down slopes having a mean inclination of 9° 26′, and with three castings where the inclination was above 12°, the proportional weight of the earth below to that above the burrows was as only 2 to 1. These several cases show how efficiently gales of wind accompanied by rain act in displacing recently-ejected castings. We may therefore conclude that even a moderately strong wind will produce some slight effect on them.

Dry and indurated castings, after their disintegration into small fragments or pellets, are sometimes, probably often, blown by a strong wind to leeward. This was observed on four occasions, but I did not sufficiently attend to this point. One old casting on a gently sloping bank was blown quite away by a strong south-west wind. Dr. King believes that the wind removes the greater part of the old crumbling castings near Nice. Several old castings on my lawn were marked with pins and protected from any disturbánce. They were examined after an interval of 10

weeks, during which time the weather had
been alternately dry and rainy. Some, which
were of a yellowish colour had been washed
almost completely away, as could be seen
by the colour of the surrounding ground.
Others had completely disappeared, and these
no doubt had been blown away. Lastly,
others still remained and would long remain,
as blades of grass had grown through them.
On poor pasture land, which has never been
rolled and has not been much trampled on
by animals, the whole surface is sometimes
dotted with little pimples, through and on
which grass grows; and these pimples consist of old worm-castings.

In all the many observed cases of soft castings blown to leeward, this had been effected
by strong winds accompanied by rain. As
such winds in England generally blow from
the south and south-west, earth must on the
whole tend to travel over our fields in a
north and north-east direction. This fact is
interesting, because it might be thought that
none could be removed from a level, grass-
covered surface by any means. In thick and
level woods, protected from the wind, castings

will never be removed as long as the wood
lasts; and mould will here tend to accumulate
to the depth at which worms can work. I
tried to procure evidence as to how much
mould is blown, whilst in the state of castings, by our wet southern gales to the north-
east, over open and flat land, by looking to
the level of the surface on opposite sides of
old trees and hedge-rows; but l failed owing
to the unequal growth of the roots of trees
and to most pasture-land having been formerly
ploughed.

On an open plain near Stonehenge, there
exist shallow circular trenches, with a low
embankment outside, surrounding level spaces
50 yards in diameter. These rings appear
very ancient, and are believed to be contem
poraneous with the Druidical stones. Castings
ejected within these circular spaces, if blown
to the north-east by south-west winds would
form a layer of mould within the trench,
thicker on the north-eastern than on any other
side. But the site was not favourable for the
action of worms, for the mould over the
surrounding Chalk formation with flints, was
only 3·37 inches in thickness, from a mean of

six observations made at a distance of 10 yards outside the embankment. The thickness of the mould within two of the circular trenches was measured every 5 yards all round, on the inner sides near the bottom. My son Horace protracted these measurements on paper; and though the curved line representing the thickness of the mould was extremely irregular, yet in both diagrams it could be seen to be thicker on the north-eastern side than elsewhere. When a mean of all the measurements in both the trenches was laid down and the line smoothed, it was obvious that the mould was thickest in the quarter of the circle between north-west and north-east; and thinnest in the quarter between south-east and south-west, especially at this latter point. Besides the foregoing measurements, six others were taken near together in one of the circular trenches, on the north-east side; and the mould here had a mean thickness of 2·29 inches; while the mean of six other measurements on the south-west side was only 1·46 inches. These observations indicate that the castings had been blown by the south-west winds from the circular enclosed space into the trench on the north-east side ; but many more measurements in other analogous cases would be requisite for a trustworthy result.

The amount of fine earth brought to the surface under the form of castings, and afterwards transported by the winds accompanied by rain, or that which flows and rolls down an inclined surface, no doubt is small in the course of a few scores of years ; for otherwise all the inequalities in our pasture fields would be smoothed within a much shorter period than appears to be the case. But the amount which is thus transported in the course of thousands of years cannot fail to be considerable and deserves attention. É. de Beaumont looks at the vegetable mould which everywhere covers the land as a fixed line or zero, from which the amount of denudation may be measured.* He ignores the continued formation of fresh mould by the disintegration of the underlying rocks and fragments of rock ; and it is curious to find how much more philosophical were the views, main-

* " Leçons de Géologie pratique, 1845 ; cinquième Leçon.' All Élie de Beaumont's arguments are admirably controverted by Prof. A. Geikie in his essay in Transact. Geolog. Soc. of Glasgow, vol. iii. p. 153, 1868.

tained long ago, by Playfair, who, in 1802, wrote, " in the permanence of a coat of " vegetable mould on the surface of the earth, " we have a demonstrative proof of the con- " tinued destruction of the rocks."[*]

Ancient encampments and tumuli.—É. de Beaumont adduces the present state of many ancient encampments and tumuli and of old ploughed fields, as evidence that the surface of the land undergoes hardly any degradation. But it does not appear that he ever examined the thickness of the mould over different parts of such old remains.   He relies chiefly on indirect, but apparently trustworthy, evidence that the slopes of the old embankments are the same as they originally were; and it is obvious that he could know nothing about their original heights.   In Knole Park a mound had been thrown up behind the rifle-targets, which appeared to have been formed of earth originally supported by square blocks of turf.   The sides sloped, as nearly as I could estimate them, at an angle of 45° or 50° with the horizon, and they were covered, especially on the northern side, with long coarse grass,

* 'Illustrations of the Huttonian Theory of the Earth,' p. 107.

beneath which many worm-castings were found. These had flowed bodily downwards, and others had rolled down as pellets. Hence it is certain that as long as a mound of this kind is tenanted by worms, its height will be continually lowered. The fine earth which flows or rolls down the sides of such a mound accumulates at its base in the form of a talus. A bed, even a very thin bed, of fine earth is eminently favourable for worms; so that a greater number of castings would tend to be ejected on a talus thus formed than elsewhere: and these would be partially washed away by every heavy shower and be spread over the adjoining level ground. The final result would be the lowering of the whole mound, whilst the inclination of the sides would not be greatly lessened. The same result would assuredly follow with ancient embankments and tumuli; except where they had been formed of gravel or of nearly pure sand, as such matter is unfavourable for worms. Many old fortifications and tumuli are believed to be at least 2000 years old; and we should bear in mind that in many places about one inch of mould is brought to the surface in 5 years or

two inches in 10 years.   Therefore in so long
a period as 2000 years, a large amount of
earth will have been repeatedly brought to
the surface on most old embankments and
tumuli, especially on the talus round their
bases, and much of this earth will have been
washed completely away.   We may therefore
conclude that all ancient mounds, when not
formed of materials unfavourable to worms,
will have been somewhat lowered in the
course of centuries, although their inclinations may not have been greatly changed.

Fields formerly ploughed.—From a very
remote period and in many countries, land
has been ploughed, so that convex beds,
called crowns or ridges, usually about 8 feet
across and separated by furrows, have been
thrown up.   The furrows are directed so as
to carry off the surface water.   In my
attempts to ascertain how long a time these
crowns and furrows last, when ploughed land
has been converted into pasture, obstacles of
many kinds were encountered.   It is rarely
known when a field was last ploughed; and
some fields which were thought to have been
in pasture from time immemorial were after-

wards discovered to have been ploughed only
50 or 60 years before. During the early
part of the present century, when the price
of corn was very high, land of all kinds seems
to have been ploughed in Britain. There is,
however, no reason to doubt that in many
cases the old crowns and furrows have been
preserved from a very ancient period.* That
they should have been preserved for very
unequal lengths of time would naturally
follow from the crowns, when first thrown
up, having differed much in height in different districts, as is now the case with
recently ploughed land.

In old pasture fields, the mould, wherever
measurements were made, was found to be
from $\frac{1}{2}$ to 2 inches thicker in the furrows than

---

* Mr. E. Tylor in his Presidential address ('Journal of the
Anthropological Institute,' May 1880, p. 451) remarks: "It
appears from several papers of the Berlin Society as to the
German 'high-fields' or 'heathen-fields' (Hochäcker, and
Heidenäcker) that they correspond much in their situation on hills
and wastes with the 'elf-furrows' of Scotland, which popular
mythology accounts for by the story of the fields having been
put under a Papal interdict, so that people took to cultivating
the hills. There seems reason to suppose that, like the tilled
plots in the Swedish forests which tradition ascribes to the old
'hackers,' the German heathen-fields represent tillage by an
ancient and barbaric population."

on the crowns; but this would naturally
follow from the finer earth having been
washed from the crowns into the furrows
before the land was well clothed with turf;
and it is impossible to tell what part worms
may have played in the work. Nevertheless
from what we have seen, castings would
certainly tend to flow and to be washed during
heavy rain from the crowns into the furrows.
But as soon as a bed of fine earth had by any
means been accumulated in the furrows, it
would be more favourable for worms than the
other parts, and a greater number of castings
would be thrown up here than elsewhere; and
as the furrows on sloping land are usually
directed so as to carry off the surface water,
some of the finest earth would be washed
from the castings which had been here ejected
and be carried completely away. The result
would be that the furrows would be filled
up very slowly, while the crowns would be
lowered perhaps still more slowly by the
flowing and rolling of the castings down
their gentle inclinations into the furrows.

Nevertheless it might be expected that old
furrows, especially those on a sloping surface,

would in the course of time be filled up and disappear. Some careful observers, however, who examined fields for me in Gloucestershire and Staffordshire, could not detect any difference in the state of the furrows in the upper and lower parts of sloping fields, supposed to have been long in pasture; and they came to the conclusion that the crowns and furrows would last for an almost endless number of centuries. On the other hand the process of obliteration seems to have commenced in some places. Thus in a grass field in North Wales, known to have been ploughed about 65 years ago, which sloped at an angle of 15° to the north-east, the depth of the furrows (only 7 feet apart) was carefully measured, and was found to be about 4½ inches in the upper part of the slope, and only 1 inch near the base, where they could be traced with difficulty. On another field sloping at about the same angle to the south-west, the furrows were scarcely perceptible in the lower part; although these same furrows when followed on to some adjoining level ground were from 2½ to 3½ inches in depth. A third and closely similar case was

20

observed. In a fourth case, the mould in a
furrow in the upper part of a sloping field
was 2½ inches, and in the lower part 4½
inches in thickness.

On the Chalk Downs at about a mile distance from Stonehenge, my son William examined a grass-covered, furrowed surface,
sloping at from 8° to 10°, which an old shepherd said had not been ploughed within the
memory of man. The depth of one furrow
was measured at 16 points in a length of 68
paces, and was found to be deeper where the
slope was greatest and where less earth would
naturally tend to accumulate, and at the
base it almost disappeared. The thickness of
the mould in this furrow in the upper part
was 2½ inches, which increased to 5 inches a
little above the steepest part of the slope; and
at the base, in the middle of the narrow
valley, at a point which the furrow if continued would have struck, it amounted to 7
inches. On the opposite side of the valley,
there were very faint, almost obliterated,
traces of furrows. Another analogous but
not so decided a case was observed at a few
miles distance from Stonehenge. On the

whole it appears that the crowns and furrows on land formerly ploughed, but now covered with grass, tend slowly to disappear when the surface is inclined; and this is probably in large part due to the action of worms; but that the crowns and furrows last for a very long time when the surface is nearly level.

Formation and amount of mould over the Chalk Formation.—Worm-castings are often ejected in extraordinary numbers on steep, grass-covered slopes, where the Chalk comes close to the surface, as my son William observed near Winchester and elsewhere. If such castings are largely washed away during heavy rains, it is difficult to understand at first how any mould can still remain on our Downs, as there does not appear any evident means for supplying the loss. There is, moreover, another cause of loss, namely in the percolation of the finer particles of earth into the fissures in the chalk and into the chalk itself. These considerations led me to doubt for a time whether I had not exaggerated the amount of fine earth which flows or rolls down grass-covered slopes under the form of castings; and

I sought for additional information. In some places, the castings on Chalk Downs consist largely of calcareous matter, and here the supply is of course unlimited. But in other places, for instance on a part of Teg Down near Winchester, the castings were all black and did not effervesce with acids. The mould over the chalk was here only from 3 to 4 inches in thickness. So again on the plain near Stonehenge, the mould, apparently free from calcareous matter, averaged rather less than $3\frac{1}{2}$ inches in thickness. Why worms should penetrate and bring up chalk in some places and not in others I do not know.

In many districts where the land is nearly level, a bed several feet in thickness of red clay full of unworn flints overlies the Upper Chalk. This overlying matter, the surface of which has been converted into mould, consists of the undissolved residue from the chalk. It may be well here to recall the case of the fragments of chalk buried beneath worm-castings on one of my fields, the angles of which were so completely rounded in the course of 29 years that the fragments now resembled water-worn pebbles. This must have been effected by the carbonic acid in the rain and in the ground, by the humus-acids, and by the corroding power of living roots. Why a thick mass of residue has not been left on the Chalk, wherever the land is nearly level, may perhaps be accounted for by the percolation of the fine particles into the fissures, which are often present in the chalk and are either open or are filled up with impure chalk, or into the solid chalk itself. That such percolation occurs can hardly be doubted. My son collected some powdered and fragmentary chalk beneath the turf near Winchester; the former was found by Colonel Parsons, R.E., to contain 10 per cent., and the fragments 8 per cent. of earthy matter. On the flanks of the escarpment near Abinger in Surrey, some chalk close beneath a layer of flints, 2 inches in thickness and covered by 8 inches of mould, yielded a residue of 3·7 per cent. of earthy matter. On the other hand the Upper Chalk properly contains, as I was informed by the late David Forbes who had made many analyses, only from 1 to 2 per cent. of earthy matter; and two samples from pits near my house contained 1·3 and 0·6 per cent. I mention these latter cases because, from the thickness of the overlying bed of red clay with flints, I had imagined that the underlying chalk might here be less pure than elsewhere. The cause of the residue accumulating more in some places than in others, may be attributed to a layer of argillaceous matter having been left at an early period on the chalk, and this would check the subsequent percolation of earthy matter into it.

From the facts now given we may conclude that castings ejected on our Chalk Downs suffer some loss by the percolation of their finer matter into the chalk. But such impure superficial chalk, when dissolved, would leave a larger supply of earthy matter to be added to the mould than in the case of pure chalk. Besides the loss caused by percolation, some fine earth is certainly washed down the sloping grass-covered surfaces of our Downs. The washing-down process, however, will be checked in the course of time; for although I do not know how thin a layer of mould suffices to support worms, yet a limit must at last be reached; and then their castings would cease to be ejected or would become scanty.

The following cases show that a considerable quantity of fine earth is washed down The thickness of the mould was measured at points 12 yards apart across a small valley in the Chalk near Winchester. The sides sloped gently at first; then became inclined at about 20°; then more gently to near the bottom, which transversely was almost level and about 50 yards across. In the bottom, the mean thickness of the mould from five measurements was 8·3 inches; whilst on the sides of the valley, where the inclination varied between 14° and 20°, its mean thickness was rather less than 3·5 inches. As the turf-covered bottom of the valley sloped at an angle of only between 2° and 3°, it is probable that most of the 8·3-inch layer of mould had been washed down from the flanks of the valley, and not from the upper part. But as a shepherd said that he had seen water flowing in this valley after the sudden thawing of snow, it is possible that some earth may have been brought down from the upper part; or, on the other hand, that some may have been

carried further down the valley. Closely
similar results, with respect to the thickness of
the mould, were obtained in a neighbouring
valley.

St. Catherine's Hill, near Winchester, is
327 feet in height, and consists of a steep
cone of chalk about $\frac{1}{4}$ of a mile in diameter.
The upper part was converted by the Romans,
or, as some think, by the ancient Britons, into
an encampment, by the excavation of a deep
and broad ditch all round it. Most of the
chalk removed during the work was thrown
upwards, by which a projecting bank was
formed; and this effectually prevents worm-
castings (which are numerous in parts), stones,
and other objects from being washed or rolled
into the ditch. The mould on the upper and
fortified part of the hill was found to be in
most places only from $2\frac{1}{2}$ to $3\frac{1}{2}$ inches in
thickness; whereas it had accumulated at the
foot of the embankment above the ditch to a
thickness in most places of from 8 to $9\frac{1}{2}$
inches. On the embankment itself the mould
was only 1 to $1\frac{1}{2}$ inch in thickness; and
within the ditch at the bottom it varied from
$2\frac{1}{2}$ to $3\frac{1}{4}$, but was in one spot 6 inches in

thickness.   On the north-west side of the
hill, either no embankment had ever been
thrown up above the ditch, or it had subsequently been removed; so that here there
was nothing to prevent worm-castings, earth
and stones being washed into the ditch, at the
bottom of which the mould formed a layer
from 11 to 22 inches in thickness.   It should
however be stated that here and on other
parts of the slope, the bed of mould often contained fragments of chalk and flint which
had obviously rolled down at different times
from above.   The interstices in the underlying fragmentary chalk were also filled up
with mould.

My son examined the surface of this hill to
its base in a south-west direction.   Beneath
the great ditch, where the slope was about
24°, the mould was very thin, namely from
1½ to 2½ inches; whilst near the base, where
the slope was only 3° to 4°, it increased to
between 8 and 9 inches in thickness.   We
may therefore conclude that on this artificially
modified hill, as well as in the natural valleys
of the neighbouring Chalk Downs, some fine
earth, probably derived in large part from

worm-castings, is washed down, and accumulates in the lower parts, notwithstanding the
percolation of an unknown quantity into the
underlying chalk; a supply of fresh earthy
matter being afforded by the dissolution of
the chalk through atmospheric and other
agencies.

CHAPTER VII.

CONCLUSION.

Summary of the part which worms have played in the history of the world—Their aid in the disintegration of rocks—In the denudation of the land—In the preservation of ancient remains —In the preparation of the soil for the growth of plants— Mental powers of worms—Conclusion.

WORMS have played a more important part in the history of the world than most persons would at first suppose. In almost all humid countries they are extraordinarily numerous, and for their size possess great muscular power. In many parts of England a weight of more than ten tons (10,516 kilogrammes) of dry earth annually passes through their bodies and is brought to the surface on each acre of land; so that the whole superficial bed of vegetable mould passes through their bodies in the course of every few years. From the collapsing of the old burrows the mould is in constant though slow movement, and the particles composing it are thus rubbed together. By these means fresh surfaces are continually exposed to the action of the carbonic acid in the soil, and of the humus-acids which appear to be still more efficient in the decomposition of rocks. The generation of the humus-acids is probably hastened during the digestion of the many half-decayed leaves which worms consume. Thus the particles of earth, forming the superficial mould, are subjected to conditions eminently favourable for their decomposition and disintegration. Moreover, the particles of the softer rocks suffer some amount of mechanical trituration in the muscular gizzards of worms, in which small stones serve as mill-stones.

The finely levigated castings, when brought to the surface in a moist condition, flow during rainy weather down any moderate slope; and the smaller particles are washed far down even a gently inclined surface. Castings when dry often crumble into small pellets and these are apt to roll down any sloping surface. Where the land is quite level and is covered with herbage, and where the climate is humid so that much dust cannot be blown away it appears at first sight impossible that there should be any appreciable amount of subaerial denudation; but worm-castings are blown, especially whilst moist and viscid, in one uniform direction by the prevalent winds which are accompanied by rain. By these several means the superficial mould is prevented from accumulating to a great thickness; and a thick bed of mould checks in many ways the disintegration of the underlying rocks and fragments of rock.

The removal of worm castings by the above means leads to results which are far from insignificant. It has been shown that a layer of earth, ·2 of an inch in thickness, is in many places annually brought to the surface per acre; and if a small part of this amount flows, or rolls, or is washed, even for a short distance down every inclined surface, or is repeatedly blown in one direction, a great effect will be produced in the course of ages. It was found by measurements and calculations that on a surface with a mean inclination of 9° 26', 2·4 cubic inches of earth which had been ejected by worms crossed, in the course of a year, a horizontal line one yard in length; so that 240 cubic inches would cross a line 100 yards in length. This latter amount in a damp state would weigh 11½ pounds. Thus a considerable weight of earth is continually moving down each side of every valley, and will in time reach its bed. Finally this earth will be transported by the streams flowing in the valleys into the ocean, the great receptacle for all matter denuded from the land. It is known from the amount of sediment annually delivered into the sea by the Mississippi, that its enormous drainage-area must on an average be lowered ·00263 of an inch each year; and this would suffice in four and half million years to lower the whole drainage-area to the level of the sea-shore. So that, if a small fraction of the layer of fine earth, ·2 of an inch in thickness, which is annually brought to the surface by worms, is carried away, a great result cannot fail to be produced within a period which no geologist considers extremely long.

Archæologists ought to be grateful to worms, as they protect and preserve for an indefinitely long period every object, not liable to decay, which is dropped on the surface of the land, by burying it beneath their castings. Thus, also, many elegant and curious tesselated pavements and other ancient remains have been preserved ; though no doubt the worms have in these cases been largely aided by earth washed and blown from the adjoining land, especially when cultivated. The old tesselated pavements have, however, often suffered by having subsided unequally from being unequally undermined by the worms. Even old massive walls may be undermined and subside ; and no building is in this respect safe, unless the foundations lie 6 or 7 feet beneath the surface, at a depth at which worms cannot work. It is probable that many monoliths and some old walls have fallen down from having been undermined by worms.

Worms prepare the ground in an excellent manner for the growth of fibrous-rooted plants and for seedlings of all kinds. They periodically expose the mould to the air, and sift it so that no stones larger than the par-

ticles which they can swallow are left in it.
They mingle the whole intimately together,
like a gardener who prepares fine soil for his
choicest plants.   In this state it is well fitted
to retain moisture and to absorb all soluble
substances, as well as for the process of nitri-
fication.   The bones of dead animals, the
harder parts of insects, the shells of land-
molluscs, leaves, twigs, &c., are before long
all buried beneath the accumulated castings of
worms, and are thus brought in a more or
less decayed state within reach of the roots
of plants.   Worms likewise drag an infinite
number of dead leaves and other parts of
plants into their burrows, partly for the sake
of plugging them up and partly as food.

The leaves which are dragged into the burrows as food, after being torn into the finest
shreds, partially digested, and saturated with
the intestinal and urinary secretions, are commingled with much earth.   This earth forms
the dark coloured, rich humus which almost
everywhere covers the surface of the land
with a fairly well-defined layer or mantle.
Von Hensen[*] placed two worms in a vessel

[*] 'Zeitschrift für wissenschaft. Zoolog.' B. xxviii. 1877, p. 360.

18 inches in diameter, which was filled with sand, on which fallen leaves were strewed; and these were soon dragged into their burrows to a depth of 3 inches. After about 6 weeks an almost uniform layer of sand, a centimeter (·4 inch) in thickness, was converted into humus by having passed through the alimentary canals of these two worms. It is believed by some persons that worm-burrows, which often penetrate the ground almost perpendicularly to a depth of 5 or 6 feet, materially aid in its drainage; notwithstanding that the viscid castings piled over the mouths of the burrows prevent or check the rain-water directly entering them. They allow the air to penetrate deeply into the ground. They also greatly facilitate the downward passage of roots of moderate size; and these will be nourished by the humus with which the burrows are lined. Many seeds owe their germination to having been covered by castings; and others buried to a considerable depth beneath accumulated castings lie dormant, until at some future time they are accidentally uncovered and germinate

21

Worms are poorly provided with sense-organs, for they cannot be said to see, although they can just distinguish between light and darkness; they are completely deaf, and have only a feeble power of smell; the sense of touch alone is well developed. They can therefore learn little about the outside world, and it is surprising that they should exhibit some skill in lining their burrows with their castings and with leaves, and in the case of some species in piling up their castings into tower-like constructions. But it is far more surprising that they should apparently exhibit some degree of intelligence instead of a mere blind instinctive impulse, in their manner of plugging up the mouths of their burrows. They act in nearly the same manner as would a man, who had to close a cylindrical tube with different kinds of leaves, petioles, triangles of paper, &c., for they commonly seize such objects by their pointed ends. But with thin objects a certain number are drawn in by their broader ends. They do not act in the same unvarying manner in all cases, as do most of the lower animals; for instance, they do not drag in leaves by their foot-stalks, unless the basal part of the blade is as narrow as the apex. or narrower than it.

When we behold a wide, turf-covered expanse, we should remember that its smoothness, on which so much of its beauty depends, is mainly due to all the inequalities having been slowly levelled by worms. It is a marvellous reflection that the whole of the superficial mould over any such expanse has passed, and will again pass, every few years through the bodies of worms. The plough is one of the most ancient and most valuable of man's inventions; but long before he existed the land was in fact regularly ploughed, and still continues to be thus ploughed by earth-worms. It may be doubted whether there are many other animals which have played so important a part in the history of the world, as have these lowly organised creatures. Some other animals, however, still more lowly organised, namely corals, have done far more conspicuous work in having constructed innumerable reefs and islands in the great oceans; but these are almost confined to the tropical zones.

INDEX.

CPSIA information can be obtained at www.ICGtesting.com
Printed in the USA
BVOW05s1725160115

383450BV00003B/50/P